P9-CQM-062

Before You Say "I Do"®

DEVOTIONAL

✦

H. NORMAN WRIGHT

HARVEST HOUSE PUBLISHERS
EUGENE, OREGON

Cover by Dugan Design Group, Bloomington, Minnesota

BEFORE YOU SAY "I DO"® DEVOTIONAL

Copyright © 2003 by H. Norman Wright
Published by Harvest House Publishers
Eugene, Oregon 97402
www.harvesthousepublishers.com

Library of Congress Cataloging-in-Publication Data
Wright, H. Norman
   Before you say "I do" devotional / H. Norman Wright
        p. cm.
Includes bibliographical references.
   ISBN 978-0-7369-0922-8 (pbk.)
   ISBN 978-0-7369-3107-6 (eBook)
   1. Marriage—Religious aspects—Christianity. I. Title.
BV835 .W735 2003
242'.644—dc21   2002012589

Printed in the United States of America.

13   14   15   16   17   / VP-CF /   20   19   18   17   16

GRAVE EXPECTATIONS

※ ※ ※

Let no one seek his own, but each one the other's well being.

1 CORINTHIANS 10:24 NKJV

Let each of you look out not only for his own interest, but also for the interest of others.

PHILIPPIANS 2:4 NKJV

*E*xpectations. Oh, you have them. And so does your fiancé. You may already be aware of them or you've yet to experience a plateful of surprises.

For many couples, their expectations remain unspoken. Many of them are desires. Some reflect a dream or an ideal rather than a necessity. Often, they turn into assumptions, "My partner should know what I need"—which never works.

Let's face it. We're all selfish. We have a "me" attitude about life. We've learned to focus on "what I want, what I can get, and what the other person (in this case fiancé) is going to do for me." This attitude runs counter to what your new married life is to behold.

See how author Gary Smalley learned this important marriage lesson:

> He was in seminary, was engaged in ministry as a youth pastor, and was in his second year of marriage to Norma. At that time, it was dawning on him that marriage was perhaps not all he thought or hoped it would be. Disagreements and conflicts were increasing. Then he went to a seminar and heard a message that, as he told the story, changed his life. The point that hit home was this: if you are irritated by

many things in a relationship, perhaps you are fundamentally self-centered and primarily looking out for your own interests.

Gary had a revelation of sorts about how he had been treating Norma. He expected her to respond to his various needs on his timetable and in the way he wanted.

If you are familiar with Gary's work, you know he has a gift for expressing the needs of the soul in graphic word pictures. Upon realizing the depths of his selfishness, he held a funeral service for himself. As he told the story, he got down on his knees—just God and Gary—and prayed, imagining his casket, funeral songs, and being laid to rest in a deep hole in the ground. Six feet under. From there, he felt led to systematically give up to God various things that he held dear. He began to see just how much he had expected everything to go *his* way in their marriage—from the car they drove to the apartment they lived in to the priority placed on his work to about what they ate for dinner. Gary said of himself following this event, "I wasn't the same any longer. Things were changing about me that I would never have imagined."[1]

If you were to hold a funeral service for some of your expectations what would you bury? It's something to think about.

Questions for Commitment

For You: Describe two or three examples of how you will put these verses into practice once you are married.

For You and Your Fiancé: Discuss what each of you would bury about your past and your expectations if you were to have a funeral service for yourself.

For God: Ask God to show you which expectations are realistic and which need to be discarded. Ask Him to give you opportunities to put into practice these passages of Scripture this week.

VOWS

❧ ❧ ❧

Lord, who may go and find refuge and shelter in your
tabernacle up on your holy hill? Anyone who leads a
blameless life and is truly sincere. Anyone who refuses
to slander others, does not listen to gossip, never harms
his neighbors, speaks out against sin, criticizes those
committing it, commends the faithful followers of the
Lord, keeps a promise even if it ruins him, does not crush
his debtors with high interest rates, and refuses to tes-
tify against the innocent despite the bribes offered him—
such a man shall stand firm forever.

PSALM 15:1-5 TLB

*M*arriage is a relationship of promises. "Promise me" is a common request from parents and friends alike.

As you grew up, you might have learned to "use" promises yourself: "I promise…really," or "Hey, *you promised!*" or "Please promise me you won't tell." Promises eventually become an important part of friendships, showing trust. You even might have exchanged a promise ring with a special friend.

Simply stated, a promise is an agreement to do something or not to do something.

When you make a promise, you're saying, *"Trust me. You can depend on me. I will follow through."* It's not just an agreement on your part, it's a commitment. And until this point, every promise volunteered on your part—whether freely given or asked of you—was just the prelude to the promise you are going to make on your wedding day.

The details of a wedding ceremony—the processional music, the attendants, the seating of the parents, the flowers, the words of the minister, the food at the reception—are important, but you could have all of the above and still not be married. *The heart of your wedding will be your vows!* Sadly, I've counseled many couples that never gave any thought to the vows until either the rehearsal or the actual wedding.

It's not just making your wedding memorable with heartfelt vows—these words will express what you will be doing with the rest of your life together!

The language of a wedding service should be the language of promising. That's why the ceremony has such a serious ring to it. The promises are to be spoken seriously and without coercion. And once you make these promises through the exchanging of vows, you and your spouse will never be the same. You will move to a new life status by virtue of your promising. A transformation will take place. What was separate before will now become "one flesh." And no matter what happens, this fact can never be erased.

QUESTIONS FOR COMMITMENT

For You: What are three promises that you will make to your fiancé?

For You and Your Fiancé: Discuss promises that each of you have made in the past and how you have honored them.

For God: Ask Him to help you discover the promises that each of you will make to one another, as well as to the Lord, when you marry.

I Promise

❧ ❧ ❧

Keeps a promise even if it ruins him.

<small>PSALM 15:4 TLB</small>

*P*romises have a future quality about them as well. A promise is only kept when it's fulfilled. A promise is not contingent upon changes in the future. It's not "I promise, if…"

There are no conditions. This is not a contract. A contract contains conditional clauses. Both parties are responsible for carrying out their part of the pact. There are conditional or "if" clauses. If you do this, the other person must do this, and if the other person does this, you must do this. But in the marriage relationship there are no conditional clauses. It's an unconditional commitment. And each day of your marriage you will need to renew your act of commitment to your partner.

Have you considered what you will promise one another? Have you considered what you are committing yourself to?

A Christian marriage goes beyond an earthly partnership. It's a commitment involving three individuals—husband, wife, and Jesus Christ.

"One standing alone can be attacked and defeated, but two can stand back-to-back and conquer, three is even better, for a triple-braided cord is not easily broken" (Ecclesiastes 4:12, TLB).

A promise is a binding pledge, a pledge of mutual fidelity and mutual submission. It is a private pledge you also make public. It is a pledge carried out to completion, working through any roadblocks. It is a total giving of oneself to another person.

Consider these vows:

Bride:

> I believe in you, (name). I want to help make all your dreams come true. I have seen your love for God, and I promise to support your decisions and submit to your leadership knowing you always seek God's will. I promise to be faithful, and I will never leave you.

> You are my best friend. I will pray for you daily, and I will always seek to grow closer to God. My desire is to be the woman you need me to be. I will make our home a place of rest, and I will always be there for you. I will listen to you and keep what I hear.

Groom:

> I am most fortunate to have found such a wonderful woman as a life partner. I happily anticipate having you as my wife and being your husband. Marriage comes with many responsibilities and even some surprises. I eagerly look ahead to them all so that we may grow together emotionally and spiritually.

> I will be your spiritual leader: I will keep Christ at the center of our relationship so that we might have spirit-filled lives. As Paul wrote in Galatians 5:22-23, "But the fruit of the Spirit is love, joy, peace, patience, kindness, goodness, faithfulness, gentleness, and self-control," I dedicate myself to assuring our marriage will have an abundance of this fruit.

> My arms will always be open to hold, comfort, and keep you safe as long as I am here on this earth.

Questions for Commitment

For You: What are three promises you want your fiancé to make to you?

For You and Your Fiancé: Share your responses from the first question.

For God: Continue to ask God to help you discover the promises that each will make to one another as well as to Him when you marry.

(For help in creating your wedding vows see *The Complete Book of Wedding Vows,* by H. Norman Wright, Bethany House, 2001.)

The Phantom
in Your Marriage

❧ ❧ ❧

Finally, brothers, whatever is true, whatever is noble,
whatever is right, whatever is pure, whatever is lovely,
whatever is admirable—if anything is excellent or
praiseworthy—think about such things.

PHILIPPIANS 4:8

*D*uring World War II, the American Forces in France had a phantom military outfit—a group called the Twenty-Third Headquarters Special Troops. With careful staging and show-business theatrics, they impersonated real troops and created an illusion of military strength to strategically fool the Germans. For example, to mask the true location of their real troops, they created fake tanks and other equipment that looked real from the air. These were phantoms.

Were you aware that many men and women bring phantoms with them into marriage? Their phantoms are mental images they think they need to battle. Their partner can't see these phantoms; only the individuals who create them are aware of them—but they seem real nevertheless.

One such phantom is an unattainable standard by which we measure our own performance, ability, looks, and characteristics. It's good to have a goal to aim for because it gives us motivation. But a phantom is an illusion, an apparition, or only a resemblance to reality.

What's the picture you have of how you should act as a husband or wife? Is this image so perfect, so idyllic that it's unattainable? Maybe. And because you can't meet those standards, what's the result?

The greater the distance your phantom is from reality, the more frustrating it will be to you. You live in its shadow. It may be confusing for your partner, who is unaware of its presence. He or she is left wondering why you seem dissatisfied and unhappy. Your future spouse might begin thinking, "Is it me? Is there something I'm doing or not doing that's creating this dissatisfaction?" Phantoms can derail marriages.

When the word "husband" comes to mind, what images pop into your mind? Who are some husbands that you know that you admire?

When the word "wife" comes to mind, what images pop into your mind? Who are some wives you know that you admire?

Questions for Commitment

For You: What are your own expectations that you have as a future wife or husband? Spend some time reflecting on where these came from. Are they realistic and attainable or do you need to make some adjustments?

For You and Your Fiancé: Discuss what each of you expects from yourself and the other in your husband/wife roles.

For God: Ask God to show you what He wants you to become as a husband or wife. Which passages from the Scripture would help you in this process?

WHAT ARE
YOU WORTH?

❧ ❧ ❧

*The Lord your God has chosen you out of all the
peoples on the face of the earth to be his people, his
treasured possession.*

DEUTERONOMY 7:6

You are…a people for God's own possession.

1 PETER 2:9 NASB

*A*s you journey into marriage, what are you worth? What
are your possessions worth? Go ahead, take a guess. You
may be surprised. Many are amazed when they itemize what they
have. There's a new show on television that has no action or vio-
lence or plot. It's held in a simple, large convention hall. People
come to have a possession appraised. Some go away ecstatic;
others are dejected. You might own a lot or owe a lot. There's a
big difference.

Possessions of those who are famous or wealthy can grow in
value to the point of being priceless. Would you pay $21,000 for
Napoleon's toothbrush? I wouldn't. But a collector did—that
much for a cruddy, old, used toothbrush. Someone else paid
$150,000 for Hitler's car. At the auction of Jackie Kennedy
Onassis' personal belongings, someone paid $211,500 for her
imitation pearls. Were they worth it? No, not really. But they were
to someone because they once belonged to someone significant.

If these items had human qualities, like a mind or emotions,
they'd probably feel quite good to know that someone wanted

them that badly. They'd feel special because they were chosen to be special.

You've been chosen to be special by your fiancé. Did you ever think about that? He or she said, "I want to be with you for the rest of my life. I'm willing to pay a price for you." It feels good to be a special possession, doesn't it?

All of us have been chosen. We are a people for God's own possession. What did we cost? It was a high price. In fact, the ultimate—the blood of Jesus. We were bought with a price, so the next time you look at your partner remember this: You don't own that person, God does (He owns you, too), and your partner was so valuable God sent His son to die for him or her (and for you, too).

Questions for Commitment

For You: Have you shared with your fiancé what he or she could do to continue to help you feel chosen? What will you do to help your fiancé feel chosen?

For You and Your Fiancé: Spend time sharing how the other has helped you to feel chosen. Thank them for doing this.

For God: Read aloud these Scriptures and thank Him for what He has done.

> Long ago, even before he made the world, God chose us to be his very own. Through what Christ would do for us; he decided then to make us holy in his eyes, without a single fault—we who stand before him covered with his love. His unchanging plan has always been to adopt us into his own family by sending Jesus Christ to die for us. And he did this because he wanted to! Ephesians 1:4,5 TLB.

YOU'RE GOING TO BE AN AUTHOR

⁂

Then the Lord God made a woman from the rib he had taken out of the man, and he brought her to the man. The man said, "This is now bone of my bones and flesh of my flesh; she shall be called 'woman' for she was taken out of man." For this reason a man will leave his father and mother and become united with his wife, and they will become one flesh.

GENESIS 2:22-24

*E*veryone who marries ends up writing a story—their own marriage story. The problem is, a husband and wife don't realize they've been writing their story until much of it has already been written. And by that time they can't go back and do any rewriting or editing. Often they discover a number of scenes they wish they could rewrite. I've heard a number of couples say, "If only I could go back I would do this or that differently" or "I would or wouldn't have said…" Many couples have difficulty just getting along. Even in the Bible we see this happening.

There are dozens of biblical tales about husbands and wives who simply couldn't get along.

- The Song of Solomon is one of the most graphic depictions of love and romance in Scripture, yet the end of Solomon's story is tragic in a spiritual sense. He eventually accumulated seven hundred wives and three hundred concubines. (That's right. He had an average of two to three anniversaries to keep up with *every day*). But this many wives turned his heart away from the Lord and to other gods. (1 Kings 11:1-13)

• King David was chastised by wife Michal for what she felt was too jubilant a display of joy and worship. Michal died childless as a result of her scorn. (2 Samuel 6:14-23)

• When Job was hit with physical, emotional, and spiritual crises (all at the same time), the best advice his loving wife could offer was, "Curse God and die!" (Job 2:9)

• Isaac and Rebekah each had a favorite son. The rivalry became so intense that Rebekah helped Jacob pass himself off as the other son, Esau, to receive a blessing under false pretense. (Genesis 27)

• Even Abraham, perhaps the Bible's premier example of faith, twice tried to pass off his wife as his sister while in a foreign country. His fear for his life apparently exceeded his love for his wife. (Genesis 12:10-20; 20)[2]

It's kind of scary, isn't it? Well, why don't you begin writing your own marriage story now? Instead of just letting it unfold, why not determine what you want it to be and what you want it to reflect? You will need to do some editing and perhaps even some rewrites along the way. Instead of waiting to see your marriage *has* unfolded, give it more direction. Be intentional. But the three of you need to do it together. Three? Yes, three. Jesus Christ needs to be at the heart of your marriage. Let Him lead. After all, He knows the path better than either of you. Remember a great marriage isn't a dream. It's a choice.

QUESTIONS FOR COMMITMENT

For You: Describe what you want your marriage to be like in four years.

For You and Your Fiancé: Share your descriptions with each other. Ask each other how you think Jesus will make a difference in your everyday life.

For God: Ask Him to show you even now areas that need to be refined so that the story line you have can become a reality.

TWO SOLVABLE PROBLEMS

≯ℓ ≯ℓ ≯ℓ

*Do nothing out of selfish ambition or vain conceit, but
in humility consider others better than yourselves. Each
of you should look not only to your own interests, but
also to the interests of others.*

PHILIPPIANS 2:3-4

*H*ave you ever struggled with doing what you don't want
to do or not doing what you want? Of course. Join the
human race. It can happen more than you realize once you're
married. When this happens you'll be in good company. Paul did
the very same thing. "I do not understand the things I do. I do
not do what I want to do, and I do the things I hate" (Romans
7:15, NCV).

Why does this happen? Well…we're all basically selfish. We may
think we're ready to love and give when we marry, but none of us
have mastered the unselfish life. No matter how much you love
your fiancé now or in ten years, no matter how committed you are
to serve them, selfishness will still emerge from time to time.

Make yourself a sign in your mind that says, "No selfishness
allowed." Acts of selfishness will put distance between the two
of you. Memorize the verse above and learn to live it.

There's another problem that couples about to marry face
today more than they did thirty, twenty, or even ten years ago.
It's called speed. Speed? That's right and we're not talking about
drugs either.

How fast are you living your life? A couple of friends of mine
put it so well when they said:

In this society speed rules. In a 70-mile-an-hour speed zone, some drive 80 and want to drive faster. We click from channel to channel, and want to click faster. We get information at an alarming rate, and want to get it faster. Our parents achieved a home, car, and some land by the time they retired; we want it all before we get married. Everything is now and in a hurry. "Hurry sickness," the chronic feeling in life that there is never enough time, defines us—the microwave and Internet generations.[3]

What's your pace of life? Are you hurrying to get the wedding preparations in place or are you taking time to enjoy the process and having fun?

When you have a day with too much to do and your body begins to tense up with the pressure to work faster, do the opposite. That's right, do the opposite. Purposely go slower and delete some items from your list. There's an equation that affects those about to be married as well as those who are married. The more pressure you put on yourself to go faster, the more you will pressure your partner to work faster and the more irritable you will become. It's true. I know of no one who at the end of their life ever said, "I wished I'd gone through life faster."

Slow down. Take time to get to know your fiancé, to laugh, to have fun, to understand one another, and to love. You don't need to be infected with hurry sickness. And I don't know of any Scripture which says, "hurry up."[4]

QUESTIONS FOR COMMITMENT

For You: In what areas of your life do you pressure yourself to go faster? Why?

For You and Your Fiancé: Are there times in which you feel pressure from your fiancé to hurry? How did this impact your relationship?

For God: When God says, "Be still and know that I am God" what is His purpose in asking this?

LOVE GIVES THE
BENEFIT OF THE DOUBT

If I speak in the tongues of men and of angels, but have not love, I am only a resounding gong or a clanging cymbal. If I have the gift of prophecy and can fathom all mysteries and all knowledge, and if I have a faith that can move mountains, but have not love, I am nothing. If I give all I possess to the poor and surrender my body to the flames, but have not love, I gain nothing. Love is patient, love is kind. It does not envy, it is not self-seeking, it is not easily angered, it keeps no record of wrong. Love does not delight in evil but rejoices with the truth. It always protects, always trusts, always hopes, always perseveres. Love never fails. But where there are prophecies, they will cease; where there are tongues, they will be stilled; where there is knowledge, it will pass away. For we know in part and we prophesy in part, but when perfection comes, the imperfect disappears. When I was a child, I talked like a child, I thought like a child, I reasoned like a child. When I became a man, I put childish ways behind me. Now we see but a poor reflection as in a mirror; then we shall see face to face. Now I know in part; then I shall know fully, even as I am fully known. And now these three remain: faith, hope and love. But the greatest of these is love.

1 CORINTHIANS 13

Stephen Covey tells of an experience he had one Sunday morning while riding a subway in New York:

> People were sitting quietly—some reading newspapers, some lost in thought, some resting with their eyes closed. It was a calm, peaceful scene. Then suddenly, a man and his children entered the subway car. The

children were so loud and rambunctious that instantly the whole climate changed.

The man sat down next to me and closed his eyes, apparently oblivious to the situation. The children were yelling back and forth, throwing things, even grabbing people's papers. It was very disturbing. And yet, the man sitting next to me did nothing.

It was difficult not to feel irritated. I could not believe that he could be so insensitive as to let his children run wild like that and do nothing about it, taking no responsibility at all. It was easy to see that everyone else on the subway felt irritated, too. So finally, with what I felt was unusual patience and restraint, I turned to him and said, "Sir, your children are really disturbing a lot of people. I wonder if you couldn't control them a little more?"

The man lifted his gaze as if to come to a consciousness of the situation for the first time and said softly, "Oh, you're right. I guess I should do something about it. We just came from the hospital where their mother died about an hour ago. I don't know what to think, and I guess they don't know how to handle it either."

Suddenly I saw things differently, and because I *saw* differently, I *thought* differently, I *felt* differently, I *behaved* differently. My irritation vanished. I didn't have to worry about controlling my attitude or my behavior; my heart was filled with the man's pain. Feelings of sympathy and compassion flowed freely...Everything changed in an instant.[5]

Has this ever happened to you? It's easy to make a snap judgment without knowing all of the facts. And you will tend to do this even more the longer you're married. You can't always tell what's going on inside a person or know the why of what they're doing unless you ask. Listen with your eyes as well as your ears and refrain from thinking the worst. We think we know why our fiancé is doing what he or she is doing and often make a condemning snap judgment. "Anyone who answers without listening is foolish and confused" (Proverbs 18:13, NCV).

Perhaps following this passage and 1 Corinthians will make a difference for your marriage experience.

QUESTIONS FOR COMMITMENT

For You: What are some examples in which you made a judgment of your fiancé or someone else and were surprised to discover what was occurring in their life.

For You and Your Fiancé: Discuss the times you tend to make a snap judgment about one another as well as what you will do differently in the future.

For God: Ask Him to help you to wait, listen, and give your fiancé the benefit of the doubt.

Marriage
Involves Friendship

❧ ❧ ❧

A friend loves at all times, and a brother is born for adversity.

Proverbs 17:17

A man of many compassions may come to ruin, but there is a friend who sticks closer than a brother

Proverbs 18:24

*F*riendship provides safety. You have a safe zone where you can be who you are. It's a biblical expression of love. We call it *phileo* or *philia*.

Friends can say almost anything

Friends feel safe with friends. You know you can be yourself. Within reason, you can say whatever you want, be whoever you are, laugh at whatever you want to laugh at, be brilliant, be a clown and all the while know that you're not being judged.

Friends keep confidences

Just as friends are able to say what they want without fear of being judged, we also know there's no fear of what we say being broadcast everywhere. Friends keep confidences. I keep yours; you keep mine.

Friends counsel

When the rest of the world doesn't care that we're about to die inside, a friend does. Friends have our best interests at heart.

Friends listen
> The flip side of that last coin is that we know that our friends have our best interests at heart when they counsel us, and we listen.

Friends sacrifice
> Just as a friend is willing to take risks on our behalf, a friend often makes sacrifices for a friend. They take joy when their friend gets what he or she wants.

Friends have no hidden agenda
> Friends work to have no hidden jealousies, desires, angers, or barriers of any kind that come between them and their friend. They are always free to suggest what is simply best for the other person without reservation. Friendship is built on honesty.[6]

Take a closer look at what Proverbs states about friendship.

QUESTIONS FOR COMMITMENT

For You: Who are your closest friends? Which of their characteristics does your spouse have?

For You and Your Fiancé: In what ways do you see one another as a friend? How would you like your friendship improved?

For God: Pray that God would help you become more of a friend to your fiancé. Ask Him to help you improve the friendships in your life.

GOD "SHOWED UP"

❧ ❧ ❧

He is not far from each one of us.

ACTS 17:27

*H*ave you heard of the play *Waiting for Godot*? It's different. The story goes like this:

> Two miserable men wait for Godot (pronounced God-o) to come and help them. Every day grows worse. Their lives are gray; even the lone tree is bare and lifeless. The men are beaten and starving. They constantly argue and bicker with each other. They witness incredible cruelty inflicted by sadistic, powerful men—and do not lift a finger to help.
>
> Apparently powerless to help themselves or others, they engage in a hopeless conversation over and over again:
>
> "Let's go!" says one.
>
> "We can't," answers the other.
>
> "Why not?" is the question repeated throughout the play—always with the same frustrating reply.
>
> "We can't go. We're waiting for Godot."
>
> Godot never comes.

Waiting for Godot was written at the time of the Second World War. The cry of humankind was understandably, "Where is God?" To many experiencing the horror, grief, and unanswered prayers of that time, it seemed He was a "no show."[7]

24

Some who have been married wonder about this. They feel God is a "no show" in their marriage. But you're not married yet so perhaps this could be posed as a question for your future.

Will God "show up" in your marriage or be a "no show?" It could be a "yes" and a "no" answer.

You didn't meet by chance. What you wanted as a child was not unknown by God. He knew you in your mother's womb. Could it be God pronounced your names together even before you were born?

And God will "show up" at your wedding. He will attend your wedding. You won't see Him. You may not see all of the guests. But He will be in attendance. He will observe what you do, what you say, and how you cut your cake. He will be there blessing your marriage and your future years of adjustment. He will be there to give you guidance and comfort. So it's not a matter of God doing a "no show." He's waiting for you to show up. Sometimes the reason God is a "no show" in a marriage is the couple failed to invite Him. They live their lives each day on their own without ever talking to Him or reading His word.

When you're married, you will need God's help. Believe it. Ask Him. Remember what Paul said, "He is not far from each one of us" (Acts 27:17).[8]

QUESTIONS FOR COMMITMENT

For You: Describe a time when you thought God was a "no show" and then discovered He was there all the time.

For You and Your Fiancé: Discuss your comfort level in talking about God and what He does in your life.

For God: Ask Him to be present in each and every decision you make between now and the wedding.

CENTER STAGE

Living as becomes you—with complete lowliness of mind (humility) and meekness (unselfishness, gentleness, mildness), with patience, bearing with one another and making allowances because you love one another.

EPHESIANS 4:2 AMP

*C*enter stage—have you ever heard that expression? Probably. When someone has made it to center stage all eyes and attention are focused on them. It's a great place to be since you're in control and can call the shots. People defer to you since you're so special. There are other people around you, but they're secondary. They may even be there in a supporting role. Their job is to make you look better or make your life easier. Everyone else accommodates you.

Look at your relationship. Look at the next ten years of marriage. Will one of you be center stage? It happens in some marriages. Many marriages seem to be built primarily on one-way accommodation. It's a one-sided approach. One takes and one gives. One makes the decisions and the other fills in. Consider these future issues:

- Who will determine when and where you spend your vacations?

- Who will determine what type of car you drive (and the color)?

- Who will determine where you live?

• Who will determine if you have pets and if so what kind?

• Who will make most of the daily decisions?

The one who is center stage is the director of the scenes and activities of a marriage.

If one member of a marriage is a dynamic person in the business world and has drive, passion, and leadership skills, are these put on the back burner when he or she comes home at night? And if one spouse is in the limelight constantly, what happens to the other? Are they unseen, ignored, or unappreciated? If others serve out in the workplace it's easy to expect that at home. If one is center stage it becomes so easy to influence, dominate, and manipulate.[9]

In a Christian marriage, center stage belongs to Jesus Christ and to Him alone. Our calling is to serve, defer, and love. This is what God's Word teaches.

"Do nothing from factional motives, [through contentiousness, strife, selfishness or for unworthy ends] or prompted by conceit and empty arrogance. Instead, in the true spirit of humility (lowliness of mind) let each regard the others as better than and superior to himself [thinking more highly of one another than you do of yourselves]. Let each of you esteem and look upon and be concerned for not [merely] his own interests, but also each for the interests of others. Let this same attitude and purpose and [humble] mind be in you which was in Christ Jesus: [Let Him be your example in humility]" (Philippians 2:3-5, AMP).

QUESTIONS FOR COMMITMENT

For You: In what areas of your life have you been center stage and in which areas an accommodator?

For You and Your Fiancé: In what way has center stage or accommodation been a part of your relationship?

For God: Ask God to help you apply these passages in a new way in your relationship.

INTIMACY— A DIFFERENT KIND

֍֍֍ ֍֍֍ ֍֍֍

Be unceasing in prayer—praying perseveringly.
1 THESSALONIANS 5:17

*M*arriage is built on intimacy. It's like a house. Those built just on human love and human intimacy are like two of the houses in the Three Little Pigs. In time, the huffs and puffs of the pressures and problems of life blow them down. If you want a lasting enjoyable marriage, build it on a substance like concrete and steel and spiritual intimacy. (Before you proceed go to the end of this devotional and answer the first two questions.)

Now that you've considered your beliefs about spiritual intimacy, here is a definition by Steve and Valerie Bell from their book *Made to Be Loved:*

> Spiritual intimacy is the satisfying connectedness that occurs when a husband and wife learn to access God and experience Him together on the deepest levels.[10]

But let's get pragmatic. What will this intimacy do for you as a couple? There are many benefits to spiritual intimacy:

- Helps build a safe environment for the greatest growth possible for you as an individual and a couple.

- Accesses God's resources of love, grace and forgiveness in your marriage (which we all need).

- Invites God into your home to restore some of the Garden of Eden's before-the-fall joy and comfort that Adam and Eve once experienced in God's presence.

- Alters your perspective about your spouse-to-be.

- Redirects you toward God as the greatest source of the love you need. This will also release you from your unrealistic expectation about being "perfectly" matched (which you will soon discover!).

- Will improve every dimension of intimacy in your relationship. The potential for the best and most fulfilling sex life is built on spiritual intimacy.

- Brings you into the best and highest level of connecting and relating to one another that you could possibly imagine.[11]

Why not interview several couples whom you admire to discover what they do to build spiritual intimacy in their marriage?

2UESTIONS FOR COMMITMENT

For You: If you had to define spiritual intimacy for someone else how would you describe it?

For You and Your Fiancé: Discuss what obstacles you may need to overcome in order to build a quality level of spiritual intimacy in the first five years of marriage.

For God: Ask God to deepen your desire for Him in your individual life with Him.

ARE YOU
REALLY PREPARED?

❦ ❦ ❦

*Lean on, trust in and be confident in the Lord with all
your heart and mind, and do not rely on your own
insight or understanding. In all your ways know, recog-
nize, and acknowledge Him, and He will direct and
make straight and plain your paths.*

PROVERBS 3:5,6 AMP

*P*reparations are the name of the game. Preparing for your
wedding is like getting ready for a trip to the wild unknown.
Think about it—what's the most important item for the wedding
itself? Is it the flowers, the place of the wedding, the photos and
video or the music? As important as these things are, they don't com-
pare with the one thing that can be reasonable or very expensive
and can set the whole tone for the wedding—the dress. In a book
written in 1912, *Why Women Are So,* the author said, "A trousseau
was as essential to the prospective bride as an outfit to the explorer
of Arctic or tropical wilds…" Are we beyond this? Listen to this:

> The wedding dress is still a big deal. Big enough to
> create a stampede at the Filene's bargain basement
> wedding dress sale. You may have heard of this rough-
> and-tumble ritual that happens each year beneath the
> streets of Boston.
>
> On the single day of the sale, hundreds of prospective
> brides from around the country descend on the depart-
> ment store. Within seconds of the store's opening,
> they have scavenged all 800 dresses off the racks.
> Without a modicum of modesty, the brides-to-be strip

to their underwear in the middle of the store, tug on white gowns, and elbow in at the mirrors. Zippers get stripped, hems get soiled, lace gets torn. But the dresses at Filene's are so cheap that no one cares about the later costs of alterations and cleaning. The object is simply to find the dress of one's dreams and get one step closer to being ready for the wedding.[12]

Everyone wants to be totally prepared for the wedding. Don't you? Of course. But will you be just as prepared for your marriage? Being prepared for a wedding is not the same as being prepared for marriage. Your wedding is over in a few hours but your marriage is meant to last a lifetime. Wedding plans are tangible and perhaps easier to work on. But marriage plans involve so much. Wedding readiness is one thing. But what about personal readiness and relational readiness?

What's *personal readiness*? It's knowing and liking who you are, having maturity and independence from your family of origin.

Relational readiness involves knowing your future spouse for at least one to two years, having a stable, growing relationship, and a similarity of values, beliefs, and attitudes. That's not asking too much, is it? Talk about this. And better yet, include God in your discussion.

QUESTIONS FOR COMMITMENT

For You: Describe how ready you feel for a lifetime of marriage both personally and relationally. What could you do to improve this?

For You and Your Fiancé: What is the most important feature of the wedding ceremony for each of you? To what degree (on a scale of 0 to 10), do each of you feel ready for marriage?

For God: Ask God to help you see beyond the romance and your feelings and identify any of the areas that are not as strong as they need to be for the marriage you want and God desires.

WHAT ARE
YOU FORGETTING?

*...forgetting what lies behind and straining forward to
what lies ahead.*

*"For I know the plans I have for you," declares the Lord,
"plans to prosper you and not to harm you, plans to give
you hope and a future."*

*L*et's see, am I forgetting something?" This is a big question couples have about the wedding and being married. The chances are quite good that you are! Most forget something. It's not the end of the world if you forget some detail about the wedding, but it is if you forget something about being married! There's a *big* difference. I've actually seen couples put so much time and energy into planning for the wedding and honeymoon (future events) that they forget a very important item—saying goodbye to their former single life.

Right now your emphasis is focused on what you will get or what you will receive as wedding gifts as well as being married. That's normal. It's exciting. I've seen people keep lists of what they will be receiving as well as what they want. But I've never seen a list of what they'll be giving up. You see, there's a lot you need to say goodbye to when you get married. Some of your personal habits will undergo a change as well as your activities. Just believe me on this one. It *will* happen. If it doesn't, well, let's not even go there! If you just tossed and dropped your clothes wherever you felt led and Mom picked them up for you, that's not going to happen anymore. That is, unless you invite your mother to come live with you. Playing basketball three nights a week or going out with friends from work may not fit into your marriage.

Perhaps you've lived with roommates for three years. That's familiar and you're accustomed to that pattern. It's true you're looking forward to a new permanent roommate but leaving those relationships involves saying goodbye. It's a loss. And losses need to be grieved.

And speaking of friends, you may not be leaving your closest friends behind but the amount of time you spend with them or even talk with them may change significantly. That too is a loss.[13]

David and Claudia Arp suggested:

> While some aspects of singleness may be easily relinquished others may be harder to give up. Of course you don't have to completely eliminate your relationships or some of your solitary activities, but you will surely need to change many things about the way you now live. So instead of being surprised by how your life will change, identify the habits and activities you know need to end and bid them a fond farewell. You can make a creative ceremony out of saying goodbye, develop a "twelve-step plan" for breaking a bad habit, or overindulge in the activity as a final blitz. But take charge of the process and put closure on your past now, when you have the time and the ability to say goodbye in your own way. After you are married, you may be so consumed with building your new life that you may resent the sudden changes in habit you hadn't prepared for.[14]

It may help to remember God's promise mentioned at the beginning of this devotional.

QUESTIONS FOR COMMITMENT

For You: What do you think will be the most difficult to leave behind from your single life?

For You and Your Fiancé: Discuss what you think will be the biggest adjustment for your fiancé regarding something from their past.

For God: Ask God to help you identify what you need to change from your past that you may not even be aware of at this time.

Have a Good
First Year

❦ ❦ ❦

I, therefore, the prisoner for the Lord, appeal to and beg
you to walk (lead a life) worthy of the [divine] calling
to which you have been called—with behavior that is
a credit to the summons of God's service.

EPHESIANS 4:1 AMP

*R*ecently a couple in their mid-twenties shared this experience with me. They were supposed to attend a big
Thanksgiving get-together, but the woman became quite ill, so
she and her fiancé couldn't go. He came over and stayed around
the clock for four days just helping her recover. Following the
experience she said, "I was so surprised at his patience and sensitivity. I saw a new side to him that I didn't know was there. It
was so reassuring."

This couple is well on their way to preparing for a great first
year of marriage. They had taken the time to get to know each
other well. They were committed to each other and to the goal
of their future marriage. And their commitment and caring had
stood up under several tests, including this illness.

Unfortunately, not all couples are so well prepared.

"I'm singing the blues." It's a line you would expect to hear
from a cabaret singer, not a newlywed. After all, marriage is supposed to be the promised land where happiness abounds. Perhaps, but perhaps not.

About her first year of marriage a wife said, "The first year of our marriage was a disaster, at least for me. John wasn't anything like my father. When we were dating, in his eyes I couldn't do anything wrong. After the honeymoon, I couldn't do anything right. He didn't like this, he didn't like that. And he is blunt and direct—no tact! There was no joy in marriage. What did I do wrong?" She was singing the "Wedding Bell Blues." Disappointment, not happiness, was her prevailing feeling.

Is this normal? After the honeymoon, is this what to expect? Every couple will experience an adjustment after the honeymoon is over, and they settle into the first year of marriage.

When you are dating and in the courtship phase, you idealize each other. You're eager to find someone who shares your dreams, your goals, and your outlook on life. You focus on your similarities, what you have in common, and you pay little attention to your differences unless they are especially annoying. Love is blind, and even if you are aware of some bothersome qualities in your partner, you may not want to see them. So you overlook them because we're always supposed to look for the best in the other person, aren't we?

Another problem affects most couples—you either attribute to your fiancé special traits or qualities you wish were there (and really aren't), or he behaves in such a way to make you believe that's the way he is, when in reality, he isn't. This is called "courtship deception." Are you getting what you think you're getting, or not?

Many couples based their decision to marry on physical love. This carries a marriage for about three to five years. Some based their marriage upon romantic love. This may carry a marriage along for five to seven years. If friendship love and agape love haven't developed, the relationship feels empty.

You can expect your physical attraction and romantic attraction to fade. That's normal. The lasting marriages are the ones where the couples built their love upon friendship and sacrificial love. In some ways, it's not really love that will hold your marriage together—it's commitment. This is a binding pledge or promise not only to the other person but to the marriage itself.

Commitment means giving up childish dreams and unrealistic expectations and accepting disappointments in marriage. Commitment means seeing your future spouse as a friend.

As you approach marriage, take plenty of time now to get acquainted and build a quality friendship. The more you do now, the more prepared you will be to experience a great first year of marriage.

QUESTIONS FOR COMMITMENT

For You: What do you think might be your biggest adjustment or even disappointment during the first year of marriage?

For You and Your Fiancé: In what way could the two of you build your friendship as well as sacrificial love for one another?

For God: Ask God to help you handle the inevitable disappointments that occur in marriage. And when they occur, ask God for the words to share with your spouse that will cause your relationship to grow.

BE ONE
IN THE SPIRIT

✤ ✤ ✤

*Get rid of all bitterness, rage and anger, brawling and
slander, along with every form of malice. Be kind and
compassionate to one another, forgiving each other, just
as in Christ God forgave you.*

EPHESIANS 4:31,32

Getting along with others is not always the easiest task.
Especially when you're married. It not only takes work, it
requires the absence of four different spirits. We use the word
spirit in many ways. We say, "She's high-spirited" or "He's got an
evil spirit." The word can be used in a positive or negative way.

The *competitive spirit*. This is a sure way to contaminate a relationship. Whenever there are several people involved in any
task, you've got to work together. You get much more accom-
plished when the two of you function as partners rather than
competitors. This is hard for some of us because you may have
been raised to be a competitor. Plus we live in a competitive
society. When you're competitive you look out for yourself, dis-
parage the successes of others, and focus on winning rather than
on serving others. Can you see what that would do to your marriage? But you can do your best and live a life of excellence
without it being at the expense of others, especially your fiancé.

The *critical spirit* destroys not only the other person, but the
one possessing it. Often it comes from either being overly critical of ourselves or from being a perfectionist. No matter the

reason, it's just not a good way to live. God's Word says, "Therefore let us stop passing judgment on one another. Instead make up your mind not to put any stumbling block or obstacle in your brother's way" (Romans 14:13).

Some struggle with the *vain spirit*. We're enamored with ourselves; our calling in life seems to be to impress others. We love to look in the mirror. Have you seen the man or woman who's always checking themselves out in the mirror? It's as though they're a bit narcissistic. And the narcissist is a legend in his or her own mind. Some love to capture people's attention and live off their applause. When this spirit overtakes us, it's difficult to reflect on the presence of Jesus in our lives. The two can't live together. And it's hard for the couple as well.

The last spirit is very destructive. It's the *adversarial spirit*. When we're at odds with another person and feelings linger, bitterness and resentment come into play. In marriage we're called to be allies, not adversaries. God's Word tells us there's a better way to live. Read today's scripture again. Let the spirit of these two verses indwell your heart and run your life.[15]

ℚUESTIONS FOR 𝒞OMMITMENT

For You: Of the spirits mentioned, which is the most difficult for you to live with in another person?

For You and Your Fiancé: Discuss what you will do to keep any of these spirits from invading your marriage.

For God: Ask Him to keep you from ever developing any of these spirits and to become more of a person of compassion.

What About
Tomorrow?

Why, you do not even know what will happen tomorrow.
What is your life? You are a mist that appears for a little
while and then vanishes. Instead, you ought to say, "If
it is the Lord's will, we will live and do this or that."

James 4:14,15

*W*hat are the events that happened to you in the past that are really significant? Think about it for a minute. In the past 20 years, what are the three most significant events of your life? How did they impact you? How did they affect you spiritually? Often we get caught up in remembering the past a bit too much, and get stuck there. We spend too much time experiencing the past good times, especially if the present is kind of ho-hum. But sometimes it pays to stop and take stock of the past in order to set a course in the present.

This is especially important since you're going to be walking down the aisle in the near future. And you're bringing all of your past with you. That includes events, experiences, and memories you wish you didn't have—or that you wish you had. You're a product of all these. And some want to come to the forefront when something triggers them after you're married. And you'll wonder, *"Where did that come from?"* The experience will create a little bit of uncertainty. After all, we all want to be in control of our life, especially our future.

James has an unnerving message for each of us: Life in the future is uncertain. That means *your* future. How does that make you feel? What we have to look forward to is not the certainty of the events of the past, but the inevitability of the unexpected occurring in the future. In fact, the best-case scenario that you could imagine could occur as easily as the worst-case scenario. Life is uncertain. That's nothing new. It's always been that way.

Life is also short and challenging. We're not to live in fear of the future or constantly be asking, "What if?" Facing the future when you're married makes it less threatening. You have that to look forward to. The way Chuck Swindoll puts James 4:14,15, in perspective is great:

> *Life is challenging.* Because it is short, life is packed with challenging possibilities. Because it is uncertain it's filled with challenging adjustments. I'm convinced that's much of what Jesus meant when He promised us an abundant life. Abundant with challenges, running over with possibilities, filled with opportunities to adapt, shift, alter, and change. Come to think of it, that's the secret of staying young. It is also the path that leads to optimism and motivation.[16]

You as a couple have challenges awaiting you in the future. Face them and rejoice.

2UESTIONS FOR COMMITMENT

For You: What is your greatest concern about the future?

For You and Your Fiancé: What is your fiancé's main concern about the future for the two of you?

For God: Ask God to help you accept the uncertainty of the future as an opportunity to depend on Him.

THE MINISTRY
OF MARRIAGE

❧ ❧ ❧

You are the light of the world...Let your light so shine
before men.

MATTHEW 5:14,16 AMP

When you marry, the two of you accept a ministry. Surprised? It's true. You're called into ministry. Your first ministry of marriage is to each other—to help each other grow emotionally, socially, intellectually, and spiritually in a journey to become what God has gifted each of you to be. Couples grow emotionally by learning to give and receive care and nurture. You'll grow socially by learning all the little skills—listening, compromise, communication, conflict resolution—that make it possible to live with your partner, skills that readily translate into relationships in the larger world. You'll learn intellectually by sharing and testing ideas. You'll learn spiritually by praying for and with each other, by participating in a community of faith together, by working side by side and serving others.

If you're faithful to your first ministry, you're ready for a second ministry of marriage—ministry to children. The arrival of children almost always puts a strain on a marriage. Only if you've learned what it means to love unselfishly can you support each other as parents. For example, once a child arrives your private couple time will be cut down to ten to twenty percent of what you had. Count on it.

The third ministry of marriage is to other people. It takes a lot of work for two people to get a marriage to the point where they have something to offer as a couple to others. Those who haven't worked on the first ministries of their marriage, ministering to each other and to their children, are like an empty cup offered to a thirsty world. They have nothing to offer others.

How does this relate to you? If you and your fiancé have worked on your first ministries, it's likely you'll have something to offer to your church, your community, and your world.

Your fourth ministry of marriage will be to the world. Sometimes this ministry takes the form of organized, formal outreach projects to serve a broken world. This is an important part of the path to connecting with others spiritually.[17]

These are things to begin thinking about during your engagement.

Questions for Commitment

For You: What would you like to offer to other couples after you're married and when?

For You and Your Fiancé: What do you see your fiancé being able to offer to others ten years from now?

For God: Ask God to give you areas of ministry that you can do together as a team effort.

TRUST ME

❧ ❧ ❧

*Now faith is being sure of what we hope for and certain
of what we do not see.*

HEBREWS 11:1

rust me. It's a phrase we either totally believe or totally dis-
trust. Sometimes we say, "I wouldn't trust that person as far
as I could throw him!" Trust is a bonding card of any relationship, but especially between a couple about to marry. After all,
who in their right mind would marry anyone if they had questions about trust!

Do you know what trust gives you? It gives a sense of pre-
dictability in your relationship. Abraham knew what trust was.
He was "fully persuaded that God had power to do what he had
promised" (Romans 4:20,21). But how would *you* define trust?
What does it mean to your fiancé? How do you build it?

Trusting someone means you choose to be vulnerable to your
fiancé. Look at some of trust's characteristics:

First of all, trust can't be forced. As a couple, each of you has
to make the choice to trust the other. It's also a judgment and an
attitude. You have to be convinced that your partner is trustworthy.
Trust involves risk. It's handing off the power to control something
to someone else. If you say you trust your fiancé, but then you
check up on him or supervise what she does, that's not trust. If
you really trust, you haven't made a back-up plan in case your
fiancé lets you down. If you do, you're sending a message that you
don't really trust him or her. Sometimes couples moving toward
marriage are so caught up in the wedding plans or infatuation that

they don't consider this area. And if it's brought into question after you're married, you wonder if something has changed or you were just blind before.

When you trust, there's a cost. It means choosing to step forward with a sign on you that says, "Here I am. I'm vulnerable. Please handle me with care." Trust is fragile; it must be protected.

Trust is nothing to play with. It's serious business. As an engaged couple and soon-to-be marriage partners, your individual reliability and faithfulness send the message, "I can be trusted." You are a promise-keeper just as God is. In fact, if you want to see the ultimate trustworthy person, look at God. He's our model for marriage.[18]

Questions for Commitment

For You: In what way do I see myself as a trustworthy person?

For You and Your Fiancé: In what way do you see me as a trustworthy person? How could I improve?

For God: Ask God to show you any area of your life that He wants you to trust Him more.

WHAT WILL MAKE
YOUR MARRIAGE WORK?

❧ ❧ ❧

If anything is excellent or praiseworthy—think about
such things.

PHILIPPIANS 4:8

*I*f I held a marriage seminar with 100 couples and asked
everyone: "What are the problems and difficulties in your
marriage?" What do you think would be the outcome after
everyone shared? There would be a dark cloud of doom and
despair over all of us. Everyone would probably leave discouraged and without hope. I also doubt if many would benefit from
the time together. I'm not suggesting that we overlook or ignore
the problems—but there are better ways to solve them.

If I were to ask every couple to share what is working for them,
what a different atmosphere and outcome we would have following the meeting! Couples would be encouraged and chal-
lenged by what they heard. They would have discovered new
ways of revitalizing their own marriages.

After you're married, what will you focus on? Sometimes it's
our personality preferences that propel us to focus on the "dark"
side or it could be because we're a perfectionist. It might even
be the result of past damage in our life.

Attitude and approach make a huge difference. In baseball, for
example, even the best hitter falls into hitting slumps. They try
and try to break out of it. Many will get videos of themselves bat-
ting to see what they can learn. The videos they select will make

a major difference. Some will look at videos taken when they're in the slump. They watch their worst performances, thinking that if they focus on this they can learn what they're doing wrong and correct it. Unfortunately, this doesn't work very well. Others select older videos that show them in a hitting streak, doing fantastically. They watch and observe what they were doing that worked. Soon, they're able to get back to that level because they concentrated on what was working.

Marriage isn't all that different, and once you're married you'll have more potential for adjustments and conflicts. The best step any couple can take to solve problems is to focus on what is working. What about during your engagement? I'm sure most of the time you and your fiancé get along. Can you describe specifically what you and your fiancé do differently during the good times? Think about it. Identify it. Use it to keep on track. After you're married, celebrate and remember the times you get along. Talk about them. Learn from them. Don't concentrate on problems or they'll grow.

2UESTIONS FOR COMMITMENT

For You: What are the times we get along the best and what makes that happen?

For You and Your Fiancé: What contributes to problems and what could be done to correct that?

For God: Ask Him to show you specific Scriptures which if applied now will enrich your marriage in the future.

Are You Mature?

⊱ ⊱ ⊱

Finally, all of you, live in harmony with one another;
be sympathetic, love as brothers, be compassionate and
humble. Do not repay evil with evil or insult with insult,
but with blessing because to this you were called so that
you may inherit a blessing.

1 Peter 3:8,9

*H*ow would you apply this passage to your future marriage?
Would you say you're a mature person? Most of us would.
Are you marrying a mature person? Well, of course; no one
wants to marry a child! There are different kinds of maturity.
There's physical maturity, emotional maturity, intellectual matu-
rity, and what this passage is talking about, spiritual maturity.

Let's consider the spiritual maturity virtues in this verse as they
apply to marriage.

The first is unity or to live in harmony with one another. In
other words, get along with other people. Is there a oneness of
heart, a similarity of purpose and harmony in your relationship?
We're called to live this way with other believers, even those to
whom we're married. How do you get along with your fiancé's parents or siblings? Remember, you do end up marrying the family.

Mutual interest is the next checkpoint. "Sympathetic" means
when your fiancé is weeping, you weep. When he or she rejoices,
you rejoice. There is no competition, envy, or jealousy between
you. When your fiancé gets the attention or a better present from
his or her folks, or the raise and promotion, you rejoice with him
or her.

Friendship and affection are found in the admonition "love as brothers." Friends give comfort during a time of need. They reach out rather than wait to be called. Which one of you is quick to pick up on the fact your fiancé has had a bad day?

"Compassionate" is another virtue of spiritual maturity. How could you demonstrate compassion toward one another this week?

The next one is humility. You let others give you the praise rather than giving it to yourself. Humility means no self-promotion or spotlighting yourself. Weddings are an event when it's easy to capture the spotlight. Sometimes it ends up being a competition between entire families.

Now the last one, "don't return evil for evil," translates into "be willing to forgive." How do you know if forgiveness has occurred? Well, if you've forgiven your fiancé, you won't try to strike back or get even. You'll restrain from saying anything ugly in return. You'll do something good for your fiancé, whether you think he deserves it or not. Remember that you've been called to endure harsh treatment.

It may be easier to reflect these traits of spiritual maturity with others you don't know as well, but the real test will come when you're married.[19]

QUESTIONS FOR COMMITMENT

For You: Which of these is the most difficult trait to be consistent in living out in your life?

For You and Your Fiancé: How could each of you assist the other in following the specifics of the verse?

For God: In what way would God say (not your parents) you need to grow in the areas of maturity?

LIVE THE SCRIPTURE

✣ ✣ ✣

Therefore, as God's chosen people, holy and dearly loved, clothe yourselves with compassion, kindness, humility, gentleness and patience. Bear with each other and forgive whatever grievances you may have against one another. Forgive as the Lord forgave you. And over all these virtues put on love, which binds them all together in perfect unity. Let the peace of Christ rule in your hearts, since as members of one body you were called to peace. And be thankful. Let the word of Christ dwell in you richly as you teach and admonish one another with all wisdom, and as you sing psalms, hymns and spiritual songs with gratitude in your hearts to God. And whatever you do, whether in word or deed, do it all in the name of the Lord Jesus, giving thanks to God the Father through him.

COLOSSIANS 3:12-17

*D*o you want your love to last forever?

Do you want your honeymoon to continue for months?

Do you want to be treated by your spouse as you were during the courtship?

Do you know what we call these questions? No-brainers. That's right. Of course, your answer is yes, yes, yes!

If you want your love to last, look at how you demonstrate love to one another during this time of your life and the first three months after you marry. That's right, make a list so you can remember (not what your partner does, but what you do). If you're attentive, polite, sensitive, patient, and verbally affectionate now, why should all this change?

If you talk about how much you love one another now, why should that change? It won't if you make it a habit. Your first priority is to your new marriage partner, not a stranger. It's true, we're often more polite to others than to our spouse. Why should others get the benefit of your love? This needs to be reserved for the love of your life. Were you aware that politeness is one of the first things to go in a marriage? But it doesn't have to. It's a choice.

I know couples that make it a point each day (not week or month) to choose a special loving act they know means a lot to their spouse and then do it for them. It doesn't become routine or old. It's a demonstration of love that connects with their partner. It's also an extension of some of the attentive responses they demonstrated to one another during the courtship. Years ago I read something like this, "It was the act of doing things for and with the other person that you fell in love. It's in the act of doing things for and with the other person that you will stay in love!"

Why this passage of Scripture to start this devotional? Simple. If you will memorize it, practice living and demonstrating it to your partner as your marriage verse, all the questions at the beginning can become a reality. But it's your choice.

QUESTIONS FOR COMMITMENT

For You: Which of the behaviors in this passage is the easiest for you to do for your fiancé and which is the hardest?

For You and Your Fiancé: Discuss together how each of you would like each behavior mentioned in this passage expressed.

For God: Ask God to help you see which teaching in this passage would make you a more mature individual.

How's Your Gratitude?

≈≈ ≈≈ ≈≈

Let the peace of Christ rule in your hearts, since as members of one body you were called to peace. And be thankful.

COLOSSIANS 3:15

Gratitude is a simple word, an important word. It's one that needs to be at the heart of your marriage. Webster says gratitude is a feeling of thankful appreciation for favors or benefits received.

Colossians 3:15 tells us to be thankful—again and again. We're told in the Psalms to give thanks.

Would others describe you as a thankful person? You don't have to answer right away. Think about gratitude. It's probably easy to be thankful at this time in your life. But what about a year from now...or five or ten? How do you keep an attitude of gratitude with all the pressures you'll experience in the next few years?

Here's the usual scenario that happens in the first few years: You'll gradually focus on things that bother you or that you don't like about your partner. But it doesn't have to be that way. If something does irritate you and you feel compelled to criticize the other, go ahead. *But* follow it with sharing five compliments or expressions of gratitude. Instead of focusing on what you don't like, catch your partner doing something good! Something you like. What a difference this will make. What would happen if you

52

commented on at least five things your spouse does every day for which you are grateful? As one therapist said:

> Think of the wonderful fruit this intervention could bear in your relationship. In my own marriage, I know how well I respond when my wife acknowledges something I have done for her or compliments my appearance on a particular day. Besides making me feel good, I like pleasing her, and so I try to do those things more often. I don't think I am unique in this way. Everyone loves approval, but husbands and wives tend to be more stingy with it than they should. As a result, spouses end up feeling unappreciated by and isolated from each other.[20]

And here's something that you could begin doing now and make into a yearly tradition. Think about it:

- Write a letter to your fiancé that describes how he or she has helped you become the person you are today. Assuming you like the person you have become, thank your fiancé for helping you grow.

- Give your fiancé a "Gratitude Party." Go out to dinner and give him or her a few small gifts, each of which should represent something about him or her that you appreciate. For example, a small mirror to represent her beauty, a small handmade certificate for his being thoughtful. The gifts don't have to be expensive but each should show thoughtfulness and gratitude.[21]

We are to be a better person because of being married to our spouse...and the reverse.

QUESTIONS FOR COMMITMENT

For You: List five things you're grateful for that your parents have done for you. When is the last time you told them? Perhaps a little note to this effect would make their day.

For You and Your Fiancé: Ask one another what you're thankful for just during this past month. What have each of you neglected to thank the other for?

For God: Ask God to show you the area of your life in which you need to be more thankful and make a list of these items.

WHAT KIND OF
FOOD ARE YOU?

And become useful and helpful and kind to one another.

EPHESIANS 4:32 AMP

*W*hat's your favorite dish? What type of food do you really prefer? Some like the variety a buffet offers while others prefer the same basic food again and again. Our food tastes tell a lot about us as individuals. On the other hand, it could be that we are like certain types of food. Strange thought? Not really. Consider the following idea by Bill Farrel. He offers an interesting take on differences:

> Men and women are different! Once we understand that, we can delight in those differences. And they can draw our hearts together more intimately.
>
> When it comes to the way men and women think, we are radically different. We like to say that men are like waffles and women are like spaghetti. Let's take a look at men first. Men compartmentalize life, focusing on one thing at a time. It's like this—when you look at a waffle, you see lots of individual boxes with walls in between them. Men deal with life as if their brains contained a waffle. They take one issue and put it in a box, then take the next issue and place it in another separate box. If we could see a man's thoughts, they would look just like a waffle, with each little box holding an individual area of life. This causes men to do only one thing at a time. When men are at work, they are at

work. When men are doing yard work, they are doing yard work. When men are fishing they are fishing. And when your loved one is thinking about being intimate with you, that's all he's thinking about!

Women, on the other hand, experience life more like a plate of spaghetti. If you look at a plate of spaghetti, you immediately notice that everything touches everything else. That is how women think—they connect every issue. Women have this incredible ability to deal with everything simultaneously. Since it is impossible to fix everything and have it all under control, women fit everything in life together emotionally, feeling something about each issue in their lives. Women may feel happy emotions like sentimentality, joy, and enthusiasm, or they may feel sad emotions like depression or frustration. But the key is to experience *some* emotion. Once women have emotionally connected with each issue in their lives, they will relax and begin to enjoy the world around them. Women are terrific at combining things. In the same half hour, they can call a friend, plan a special dinner, run a business meeting, write a Christmas card, check in with the kids, and not miss a beat!

The first key to enjoying both waffles *and* spaghetti is to take turns leading the conversation. When the discussion is female-oriented, men need to get ready to take a verbal journey. Know that she will change subjects regularly and explore many ideas before the discussion is over! It's like she's traveling around a plate of spaghetti, switching directions each time two issues meet.

When the discussion is male-oriented, women need to prepare themselves to stay put and focus on the issue at hand. As a man explores the single issue that is on his mind, he will discover needs behind that issue. As he gets in touch with the needs that motivate his behavior, his lover will feel closer to him and gain satisfying insight into his life. The important thing to remember is that a man takes awhile to discover these needs on his own. He needs the help of a patient, interested partner to help him learn about himself.

It's one of the great mysteries in life. Members of the opposite sex need one another, but they don't always have the answers for each other. Men aren't women and women aren't men! But as we learn to take risks and open up to each other we will learn and grow both individually and as a couple.[22]

QUESTIONS FOR COMMITMENT

For You: Is your mind more like a waffle or spaghetti? Are the two of you the same or different? If the two of you are different how does this affect your communication?

For You and Your Fiancé: Discuss how you are similar as well as different in your thinking, decision-making, etc. What can you do to adapt better to one another?

For God: Ask Him for a greater amount of acceptance and understanding for the uniqueness of your fiancé.

YOU'RE A MIRROR

For he chose us in him before the creation of the
world to be holy and blameless in his sight.

EPHESIANS 1:4

*B*ill and Pam have been married for a number of years. Here is part of their honeymoon adjustment.

"Mirror, mirror, on the wall, who's the fairest of them all?" Our words are mirrors to another's soul. Too often we give those closest to us cracked mirrors of displeasing words or hurtful remarks. These cracked mirrors give a distorted reflection of the person. But when we reflect to those we love their uniqueness and value, they begin to see themselves as priceless.

On our honeymoon, Pam stepped out of the shower and, looking in the mirror, began putting on her makeup. While doing so, she began to verbally criticize her physical attributes. From head to toe, she complained about the way she was put together.

I was lying on the bed admiring Pam when she began her personal evaluation. Inside I was becoming frustrated—after all, she was criticizing my wife!

I got up and walked toward Pam. I wrapped my arms around her and gave her a reassuring hug. Then I stepped back, took her face tenderly in my hands, and said, "Pam, let me be your mirror. You are gorgeous! Let me reflect back to you the beautiful woman you are. If we have to throw all the mirrors in our house away, we will. From now on, I will be your mirror!"[23]

Love is like a mirror.
When you love another you become
his mirror and he becomes yours...
And reflecting each other's love
you see infinity.

LEO BUSCAGLIA

Sometimes in marriage we not only wound our partner by our words but we can end up wounding ourself. Did you even think of that? Have you ever complained to yourself about yourself? Probably. We use words like "I'm stupid or slow or inept or too short, too fat, too skinny or too bald." (By the way, there are no perfect bodies. No one is a "10" except in *their* own mind.) Sure, we can all use some improvement especially if we've let ourselves go. After all, our body is a temple of the Holy Spirit and we need to take care of it.

Remember, everyone's body is unique. And we're more than our body or our physical appearance. You and your fiancé have a value that is more than your height, weight, or appearance. How much value? Listen to this:

"For he chose us in him before the creation of the world to be holy and blameless in his sight. In love he predestined us to be adopted as his sons through Jesus Christ, *in accordance with his pleasure and will*" (Ephesians 1:4-5, emphasis added).

ǪUESTIONS FOR COMMITMENT

For You: In what area of your life do you struggle the most with self-acceptance?

For You and Your Fiancé: Discuss how each of you can encourage one another in an area in which you feel weak.

For God: Ask God to assist you in understanding and applying the passage in Ephesians to your personal life. Thank Him for the extent of His acceptance.

DO YOU REALLY UNDERSTAND?

❧ ❧ ❧

[…you are to feel for him all that reverence includes: to respect, defer to, revere him—to honor, esteem, appreciate, prize, and in the human sense, adore him, that is, to admire, praise, be devoted to, deeply love, and enjoy your husband]…In the same way you married men should live considerately with [your wives], with an intelligent recognition [of the marriage relation], honoring the woman as [physically] the weaker, but [realizing that you] are joint heirs of the grace (God's unmerited favor) of life, in order that your prayers may not be hindered and cut off. [Otherwise you cannot pray effectively.]

1 PETER 3:2B,7 AMP

*I*f you can learn the following information and follow it, you'll be light-years ahead of many couples. Remember the verse that says God made them male and female? Well, that really comes to light in marriage and especially in the area of sex. Gary and Barbara Rosberg in their book (highly recommended) *The 5 Love Needs of Men and Women* spell out these differences so well.

> God created males with a strong sex drive. Scientific study of sexual desire indicates that our sex drive is generated in our brain and that sexual desire can occur without any stimulus from outside of our body. The limbic system of the brain contains centers that enhance or stimulate sexual drive, and other centers that, when activated, inhibit it. We also know that testosterone, the primary male hormone (also found in women), plays a major role in a man's desire for sex.

Men also have the uncanny ability to compartmentalize their lives. We live in "boxes." We have a work box, a church box, a friend box, a sports box, a sex box, and so on. The sex box is always on the periphery of our lives, ready to be opened at a moment's notice. We may be worn out from work, preoccupied with pressures, or even struggling with conflict in our hearts, but we readily place each of those problems in a different (much smaller) box, separate from sex. We forget all the other boxes when we become sexually aroused.

Women, however, tend to tie all of these boxes together. Or perhaps a better way to say it is that when one box is open, they are all open. That's why open and vulnerable communication is so important for a woman, that's what helps her sort out all the rest and relax into physical intimacy.

Perhaps the most important fact you need to know is that man finds much of his own masculinity in his sexuality.

If this is so, what does a husband need from his wife?

- A husband needs his wife to initiate sex.

- A husband often struggles with feelings of inadequacy or failure.

- A husband gets discouraged when his wife does not express her passion for him.

- A husband feels as if he's not important to his wife when she doesn't take time to make love.

- A husband becomes concerned when life situations (such as depression, grief, and loss) interfere with his interest in sex.

- A husband feels loved when his wife receives him and responds to him sexually.[24]

It's true—men spell the word intimacy S-E-X. But what about a woman?

God has wired men and women quite differently. A man's sex drive is connected to his eyes; he becomes aroused visually. A wife's sex drive is connected to her heart; she is aroused only after she feels emotional closeness and harmony. A women spells intimacy T-A-L-K. When a woman is listened to, her point is validated and she is understood, then she feels a connection with her husband.

- A wife needs to experience emotional closeness.

- A wife needs to feel listened to and understood.

- A wife needs to feel as if she is the top account.

- A wife needs her husband's undivided attention.

- A wife needs her husband to demonstrate his respect for her as a person.

- A wife needs to feel a cut above other people.

- A wife needs to know that she is valuable to her husband.[25]

Were you aware of this? Have you ever talked about this? Intimacy is the bonding glue of marriage. It's more than the physical connection, that's important, but so is conversation—emotional, caring conversation. What you're reading here is just the tip of the iceberg. There's much more for you to learn, and you will...after you are married.

Questions for Commitment

For You: What questions do you have at this time about male-female differences? What have you read in this area?

For You and Your Fiancé: What do you need to ask each other to have a greater understanding of one another's needs? What is it you've been hesitant to discuss with one another?

For God: If you could ask God one question about sex, what would it be?

You're a
Gap-Filler

❦ ❦ ❦

It is not good for the man to be alone.
I will make a helper suitable for him.

Genesis 2:18

The first time God said something was not good, it had to do with man being alone. God created Adam isolated in the garden; he had no human counterpart. So God created a woman to meet his need for intimacy. In the original text, the Hebrew word for "suitable helper" means "one matching him." Adam needed someone who could complement him because he was incomplete by himself. This is one of the purposes of marriage: *to complete one another*.

Remember the original *Rocky* film? Sylvester Stallone was the main character. In this film he had a love relationship with a woman named Adrian. She was a little wallflower who worked in the pet shop. She was the sister of Pauly, an insensitive guy who worked at the meat house. His goal in life was to become a debt collector for a loan shark. He was a real winner!

Pauly couldn't understand why Rocky was attracted to Adrian. "I don't see it," he said, "What's the attraction?"

Do you remember Rocky's answer? The scriptwriters came up with not only a great response, but one that reflects Genesis 2. Rocky said, "I don't know, fills gaps I guess."

"What's gaps?"

"She's got gaps; I got gaps. Together we fill gaps."

In his simple but profound way, Rocky expressed it well. He said that he and Adrian each had empty places in their lives. But when the two of them got together, they filled those blank spots in one another. And that's exactly what God did when He fashioned a helpmate suitable for Adam. She filled his empty places, and he filled hers.

What are the gaps the two of you are filling in your relationship? Thank God for what the other is filling up.

Questions for Commitment

For You: What are the times when you feel most incomplete as a person?

For You and Your Fiancé: What do the two of you want from one another as it relates to filling a gap in your life?

For God: Ask God to help you identify areas that you aren't even aware of that need to be filled.

So What If
You're Different!

Bearing with one another and *making*
allowances because you love one another.

Ephesians 4:2 AMP

How do you feel about the fact (yes, it's a fact) that the two of you are so different? Is it a time of celebration or consternation? There is tremendous value in learning to appreciate your differences. You may want to revisit this page and share your discoveries.

In 1 Corinthians 12:14 we learn that diversity does not necessitate division, "Now the body is not made up of one part but of many." We can learn to maximize the value of our differences. Second, it is impossible to understand and appreciate who your spouse is without understanding his or her God-given uniqueness. Sure, there will be times when you ask God, "Why is my spouse so different?" It's when you turn that "why" question into: "Thank you God for that difference" that you're on your way. Consider these thoughts:

> If I do not want what you want, please try not to tell me that my want is wrong.

> Or if I believe other than you, at least pause before you correct my view.

Or if my emotion is less than yours, or more, given the same circumstances, try not to ask me to feel more strongly or weakly.

I do not, for the moment at least, ask you to understand me.

That will come only when you are willing to give up changing me into a copy of you.

To put up with me is the first step to understanding me. Not that you embrace my ways as right for you, but that you are no longer irritated or disappointed with me for my seeming waywardness.

And in understanding me you might come to prize my differences from you, and, far from seeking to change me, preserve and even nurture those differences.[26]

While the first two steps are important, the third one is critical. Not only do we need to acknowledge our differences and be willing to value them, but we also need to have a way to understand or make sense of those differences. And when you do, what a difference it will make in your marriage.

Questions for Commitment

For You: On a scale of 0 to 10, to what degree do you accept who you are?

For You and Your Fiancé: On a scale of 0 to 10, to what degree do you accept one another? Which difference is the most difficult for you to accept?

For God: Thank Him for each difference between the two of you and ask Him to give you a greater appreciation of one another.

REINTRODUCTION

❧ ❧ ❧

Better one handful with tranquility than
two handfuls with toil and chasing after the wind.

ECCLESIASTES 4:6

*I*n the book *Becoming Soul Mates,* Les and Leslie Parrott
have compiled more than 50 stories of how couples have
developed spiritual intimacy in their marriages. Here's a story to
encourage you to nurture this dimension of your relationship.

A couple we knew gave us some advice several months
before we married 23 years ago. That advice has served
us well and upon reflection is one of the main ways we
have cultivated spiritual intimacy in our relationship.

Our friends introduced us to the "principle of reintroduction." Simply put, this principle acknowledges that every day we change as individuals based
on our experiences that day. In order to build a
growing relationship as a couple, then we must make
time to "daily reintroduce" ourselves to each other. We
share the mundane and the profound. We disclose
what's going on in our lives and genuinely inquire
about each other's life.

Frankly, this was fairly easy to do when we were first
married and had few distractions. We had lots of time
for meaningful dialogue, cups of coffee, and sharing
activities together. But as children came and other
adult responsibilities began to crowd our schedules,
we were grateful we had established the habit early on

and that it still prevails. For no amount of reading the Bible and praying together genuinely builds our relationship if we haven't bared our lives with each other on a regular basis and feel convinced that we are "naked and unashamed" with each other in the fullest sense of that biblical definition of intimacy.

Now our daily reintroduction habit usually takes the form of a long walk, an extended cup of coffee (decaf now), or a long phone call if I'm out of town. But we keep very short accounts and we can testify that we depend on this habit to keep us growing, both as individuals and as a couple.[27]

QUESTIONS FOR COMMITMENT

For You: What are three goals you have for sharing time together after you're married?

For You and Your Fiancé: Discuss how you will greet one another and reconnect at the end of each workday. What do you want to hear and what don't you want to hear? Were you aware that if and when you have a child, 80 to 90 percent of the time you had together as a couple could vanish? What will you do to maintain couple time?

For God: In what way do you need to be reintroduced to Him at this time of your life?

Romance Versus
Infatuation

❧ ❧ ❧

Love endures long.

1 Corinthians 13:4 AMP

*L*ove and infatuation are quite different. What some call love is really infatuation. And if that's the case, then both it and the relationship will die. There is a blindness to infatuation that makes people see what they want to see. Later they discover that what they thought they saw is not what they got. When their infatuation dies, it's like stepping out of a plane without a parachute. The trip down is long and painful.

The longer we're married, the more we understand (hopefully!) the kind of love that binds us together when we are at our best and at our worst. As a friend put it, "There are many times when we look at each other and there is not physical or passionate response. That's okay. It's been there before and it will be there again. We're not threatened when it's not because we know that we love each other. That's permanent, lasting. And we think it's also a gift from God. And for that we rejoice."

As you begin your life together there's probably a strong sense of romantic or passionate love. That's good. And for many people that's how it begins. It can be the overture that comes before the main event—lasting love. Romance and passion are easy; *love is work*. The difference? "Romance is based on sexual attraction, the enjoyment of affection and imagination. Love is based on decisions, promises, and commitments."[28]

There is a benefit to romantic or passionate love:

> Passionate love performs a powerful service as long as it lasts. It focuses the total attention of two people on each other long enough for them to build an enduring structure for their relationship. The passion to love experience will never hold the two of them together forever. But building "enduring structures" for a relationship takes a lot of time and effort, and if two people are not attracted to one another physically, the hard work might never get done. That's another function of passionate love—the life-changing experience of being accepted and valued. Passionate love focuses a bright, positive light on each of the persons involved, and both of them fall in love not only with each other but also with themselves.[29]

QUESTIONS FOR COMMITMENT

For You: Describe how you know your love for your fiancé is love not infatuation.

For You and Your Fiancé: Discuss what's romantic to each of you. How would you like your partner to accept and value you?

For God: Thank Him together for His love and the love He has given you for one another.

THE LIES
WE TELL

᪣ ᪣ ᪣

You shall not give false testimony against your neighbor.

EXODUS 20:16

We're a country of proficient liars. We cultivate and practice telling lies. We're good at it no matter how young or how old we are. Two out of three people in our country see nothing wrong with lying.[30]

We can destroy another's reputation and cripple the ministry of a person or a church by our lies. But worst of all, we destroy ourselves before God: "The Lord detests lying lips, but he delights in men who are truthful" (Proverbs 12:22). "There are six things the Lord hates, seven that are detestable to him:...a false witness who pours out lies and a man who stirs up dissension among brothers" (Proverbs 6:16,19). And we add details that exist only in our mind.

We lie by embellishing stories we tell. We lie by leaving out portions to create another impression. We can speak the truth in such a way that it destroys—especially in a marriage. God's Word says to speak the truth in such a way that it better cements our relationships. "Speaking the truth in love, we will in all things grow up into him who is the Head, that is, Christ" (Ephesians 4:15).

We lie by bringing secrets about our past into our marriage. We're afraid of the reaction we might receive but when the secret comes to light after we're married, it's worse (and 99 percent of the secrets are discovered). Your spouse feels set up and deceived. Another variation of this is courtship deception. This is where you seemingly enjoy something during courtship or you respond in a certain way but after the wedding it's a different story. You know what I mean. During courtship you're open and share feelings or enjoy shopping or going to football games, or enjoy your fiancé's friends, etc. But what happens when the knot is tied?

We also lie by spreading gossip. You know, information that may be true—or may not be. Sometimes we're like walking supermarket tabloids. God's Word says: "The words of a gossip are like choice morsels" (Proverbs 18:8).

When lies occur in a relationship, trust vanishes. And remember the scripture, "an honest answer is like a kiss on the lips" (Proverbs 24:26) and pray: "Set a guard over my mouth, O Lord; keep watch over the door of my lips" (Psalm 141:3).

QUESTIONS FOR COMMITMENT

For You: What area of your life is it most difficult for you to be honest? What is your fear?

For You and Your Fiancé: Discuss what subjects are the most difficult for you to be totally honest with one another.

For God: Ask Him to reveal to you what areas of your life are hidden to you, to your fiancé, and to Him.

AN ARRANGED
MARRIAGE

❧ ❧ ❧

And show her honor as a fellow heir of the grace of life.

1 PETER 3:7 NASB

A wedding is one thing; a marriage is another. What a difference between the way things start in a home...and the way they continue. In his book *Secrets to Inner Beauty,* Joe Aldrich describes the realities of married life.

> It doesn't take long for the newlyweds to discover that "everything in one person nobody's got." They soon learn that a marriage license is just a learner's permit, and ask with agony, "Is there life after marriage?"[31]

You may think you'll be the exception and all will go smoothly. But will it? Marriage begins like a romantic, moonlight sleigh ride, smoothly gliding over the glistening snow. It's living together after the honeymoon that turns out to be rough backpacking across rocks and hot sand. Philip Yancey offers these insights:

> In the U.S. and other Western-style cultures, people tend to marry because they are attracted to one another's appealing qualities: a fresh smile, wittiness, a pleasing figure, athletic ability, a cheerful disposition, charm. Over time, these qualities can change; the physical attributes, especially, will deteriorate with age. Meanwhile, surprises may surface: slatternly housekeeping, a tendency toward depression,

disagreements over sex. In contrast, the partners in an arranged marriage [over half of all marriages in our international global village fit this description] do not center their relationship on mutual attractions. Having heard your parents' decision, you accept that you will live for many years with someone you now barely know. Thus the overriding question changes from "Whom should I marry?" to "Given this partner, what kind of marriage can we construct together?"[32]

What would it have been like if your marriage had been arranged? How do couples ever work it out when it's arranged? Whether it was arranged or made by choice, every marriage needs to be constructed. What kind would you like to construct? You have a choice. You can create your marriage or let circumstances and problems create it.[33]

QUESTIONS FOR COMMITMENT

For You: How would you have responded if someone else chose your fiancé and told you this is the one you're going to marry? Describe how (and why) your marriage will be different than most.

For You and Your Fiancé: Discuss what you will do in the first six months of marriage to build a quality marriage.

For God: Ask Him to give you insight and understanding to help you handle all the surprises you will experience after the wedding.

TEMPTATION IN
YOUR MARRIAGE

❧ ❧ ❧

No temptation has seized you except what is common to man. And God is faithful; he will not let you be tempted beyond what you can bear. But when you are tempted, he will also provide a way out so that you can stand up under it.

1 CORINTHIANS 10:13

*O*ne thing is as certain as death and taxes—when you're married you're going to encounter temptation. Everyone will be tempted because Satan is looking for someone to destroy. You will be tempted, and so will your fiancé, but probably in different ways.

What are some of the common ways husbands are tempted? Sexual impurity is a big one; lust is a struggle for many men. Then there's relational neglect. It's really easy to ignore a wife and avoid the time investment that's needed. Harshness and anger enter into the picture, especially when expectations are not being met or we feel out of control. Personal idolatry gets in there as well. It occurs when we begin to worship our careers, what we own, or our "toys." Anything come to mind?

Wives struggle, too. Some of them are tempted to manipulate their husbands into what they want them to be instead of relying upon God to make the changes. Some women engage in peacekeeping rather than peacemaking, but peacekeeping doesn't make the hurt disappear. Have you ever heard of simmering anger, the forerunner of resentment? It's quite common. And sometimes a woman who expresses her anger (after it builds up) confuses her husband. The two most common forms of expression for women who are angry, based on a national survey, are yelling and crying. (Does this sound familiar? How do you express anger? How would your fiancé describe your anger?)

There are other temptations in marriage, but the good news is that Jesus was also tempted—and He triumphed. When temptation comes, remember that God is your answer. Temptation gives God an opportunity to demonstrate His faithfulness. It's up to you to avail yourself of it.[34]

2UESTIONS FOR COMMITMENT

For You: What have been your greatest temptations in life? What might they be after you're married? Have you memorized this verse yet?

For You and Your Fiancé: What have been the temptations the two of you have struggled with up to this point in your relationship? What assistance do you want from your fiancé with any temptations you experience after you're married?

For God: Ask Him to show you the area of your life where you are most prone to being tempted now and in the future.

THE DEFORMITY

❦ ❦ ❦

Do not conform any longer to the pattern of this world,
but be transformed by the renewing of your mind. Then
you will be able to test and approve what God's will is—
his good, pleasing and perfect will.

ROMANS 12:2

*D*o you remember the movie *The Elephant Man?* It's the story of a deformed man who eventually achieves dignity. Although his body continued to thicken and deform, he changed by gaining a sense of personal worthiness and purpose.

There are many people today who aren't deformed in the physical sense, but they are in other ways. Some have deformed attitudes that are basically negative and pessimistic. This impacts a marriage. Fortunately, this deformation is curable. Some have habits that have been deformed into addictions. This can destroy a marriage. Fortunately, this deformation is also curable.

There is one deformity that mars every person alive. It's called sin. It's a spiritual deformation distorting our values and our minds. It can even cripple our abilities. You may not be able to see it from the outside, but it's there. The worst part is that the image of God, in which we were created, has been marred. Look around, read the paper, watch the news: results of sin's deformity are everywhere.

But, praise God, He intervened to change this deformity. It wasn't an external patch-up job either. It's called "regeneration," which means "changing." This is not anything we can bring about, it's the Holy Spirit bringing about a major renovation.

QUESTIONS FOR COMMITMENT

For You: Deformation: In what area do you still feel deformed?

Regeneration: When did you experience this step in your life?

Transformation: What area of your life needs this?

Renovation: In what way would you like to be renovated?

For You and Your Fiancé: Discuss how you will respond to one another whenever you discover a new deformity (and you will) after you're married.

For God: Ask Him to help you identify and correct any deformity that you may not be facing at this time.

BE A PEACEMAKER

Now when he saw the crowds, he went up on a mountainside and sat down. His disciples came to him, and he began to teach them, saying "...Blessed are the peacemakers, for they will be called sons of God."

MATTHEW 5:1,2,9

*T*here are a number of misconceptions about who a peacemaker is. Some think that to be peacemakers we should:

- avoid all arguments and conflict. (Were you aware that men are more likely to prefer avoidance than women when the conflict is between the two of them? It's true! Sometimes a man feels overwhelmed with a lot of words so he would rather get angry and use that to put a halt to the conflict.)

- be passive and nonconfrontational. (We're called to confront at times in our life.)

- be easygoing and let others always have their way. (If this happens in marriage, you end up with one spouse being a taker and the other a giver. That's not a good balance.)

The peace Jesus is talking about doesn't happen because of avoidance tactics. In fact, it's just the opposite. A peacemaker forces problems and settles them. In the last century, one of the old weapons used in the West was a revolver called "The Peacemaker." It served its purpose, but the peacemaking this passage talks about doesn't destroy people. But this can happen in marriage.

Look at God's Word and the emphasis on living in peace:

> If it is possible, as far as it depends on you, live at peace with everyone (Romans 12:18).

> Let us therefore make every effort to do what leads to peace and to mutual edification (Romans 14:19).

To be peacemakers, we've got to be at peace with ourselves. Peacemakers don't add fuel to the fire when there are conflicts. Peacemakers look for the positive and bring it out. They look for solution-oriented alternatives. A peacemaker knows how to arbitrate in order to settle disputes. A peacemaker watches what he or she says: "Pleasant words are a honeycomb, sweet to the soul and healing to the bones" (Proverbs 16:24).

QUESTIONS FOR COMMITMENT

For You: Would your partner call you a peacemaker? What are your peacemaking skills? What skills do you need to develop to make you a more effective peacemaker?

For You and Your Fiancé: Discuss the times in your relationship when it's easiest to be a peacemaker and when it is difficult.

For God: Ask Him to intervene when you move away from being a peacemaker and bring you back to reflecting the teaching of Jesus.

Fog Banks

❦ ❦ ❦

*For you were once darkness, but now you are light in
the Lord. Live as children of light.*

EPHESIANS 5:8

*F*og is interesting. It's made up of misty moisture that puts
a chill in the air and sometimes makes you shiver. It can
take a curl out of your hair and block your vision when you're
driving to the extent that you have to come to a stop. The sun
can be shining brightly, but you'd never know it. All you see is,
well, not much. Even sound is distorted. It seems as though
there's a heaviness in the air. It doesn't take much moisture for
the fog to bring everything to a halt. Were you aware that a dense
fog covering seven city blocks to a depth of 100 feet contains less
moisture than a glass of water?

Ships have crashed on rocks or run into reefs because of fog.
Planes have crashed into mountains.

In central California there is a type of fog called the *Tule Fog*.
It seems to rise off the ground and completely blacks out both
Highways 5 and 99. When it hits, some of the worst multi-car
accidents in California can happen.

Sometimes husbands and wives can feel as if they're floating
around in a fog bank, not knowing which way to turn. I've seen
a number of engaged couples walking around as though they
were in a fog. Sometimes it was because of the romantic high they
were on. On other occasions it was because of all the details of
the wedding as well as trying to meet all the expectations of
others. When someone is experiencing grief because of some loss

in their life they often describe it as being *in a fog*. Now and then there was gray gloom in the relationship because of tension and hassles. Sometimes a gray gloom drifts into a marriage relationship as well. When it does it may chill the love and closeness of the relationship. Or it could be there's a fog hiding the truth of who God is and what He wants for us. It happens.

Do you know what to do with fog? You can wait until it lifts, but that puts you at its mercy. Or you can drive out of it or climb above it. When you do that you have a sense of direction, light to show you the way, and warmth. We can't do much about the weather and that kind of fog. We can do a lot about the types of fog in your relationship—don't let it settle in.[35]

Questions for Commitment

For You: Describe some of the times in your life or your relationship that you've felt as though you've been in a fog.

For You and Your Fiancé: Discuss how you would like the other to respond to you when you feel as though you're in a fog bank because of either being overloaded or because of grief.

For God: Ask Him to give you direction to avoid those fog banks that are avoidable and for a way out when they aren't avoidable.

The Gift of Passion

God created man in his own image.

GENESIS 1:27

*H*ere's the question of the day: Are you a passionate person? Yes or no? Would your fiancé say you're passionate? Too much or not enough? Ask one another. Now define what *you* mean by passionate. The dictionary says it's having or showing strong feelings or resulting from, expressing, or tending to arouse strong feeling, ardent; intense; impassioned. It also means readily aroused to sexual activity: sensual.

Now some of you may be thinking, "Yes! That last part is me. I can identify with that!" Especially now! But what about the other definitions? Don't those apply as well?

Some people say, "Hey, I'm just not wired for all that emotion stuff. That's not me." Well, here's another question: Were you created in the image or likeness of God? The answer is yes, because we all were. Where do we get our capability to experience emotions? Where do we get the capacity to love, hate, grieve, and weep? We received this from God. Our God is a God of passion.

Perhaps you never thought of God as passionate. We know He loves. We see this in John 3:16, "For God so loved the world..." We know He hates because Proverbs 16:16 talks about seven things God finds detestable: "haughty eyes, a lying tongue..." We know He laughs: "He who sits in the heavens laughs" (Psalm 2.4, NASB). We know He cries: "Jesus wept" (John 11:35). The Scripture tells us God embraces, kisses, shouts, whispers, sings, and grieves (see Luke 15:20; Jeremiah 25:30; 1 Kings 19:12; Zephaniah 3:17; 1 Chronicles 21:15).

83

Our emotions are good even though we may not understand them. If you're more reserved and your fiancé is expressive, you may have conflicts over this. Even though women are wired to experience emotions and encouraged to do so more than men, both sexes were created to be people of passion. If one of you hasn't yet developed your understanding and expression of your emotions, let it unfold. It may be uncomfortable, but it will enrich your life—and your future marriage.

QUESTIONS FOR COMMITMENT

For You: What are five emotions that you experience and express readily and what are five emotions that your fiancé experiences and expresses.

For You and Your Fiancé: Discuss how each of you feels about expressing emotion in front of the other. Which emotions do you struggle with? What could the other do to assist you in becoming more of a person of passion?

For God: Ask Him to show any emotions that you've blocked in your life and that need to come to the forefront.

Guidelines for Your Marriage

*Be kind and compassionate to one another, forgiving
each other, just as in Christ God forgave you.*

EPHESIANS 4:32

*Trust in the Lord with all your heart and lean not on
your own understanding; in all your ways acknowledge
him, and he will make your paths straight.*

PROVERBS 3:5,6

The following statements all have the same ingredient in
common—they work to enrich your marriage. Consider
following these in your marriage to reflect your commitment to
one another and the Lord:

- Don't compete with one another—be a friend. Wish your
  partner the best and be enthusiastic about their achieve-
  ments—in private as well as in public.

- It's not your job to *reform* your partner. You're called to
  be an encourager. Leave the work of transformation up
  to the Holy Spirit.

- Ask your partner what three words they'd like you to drop
  from your vocabulary—then do it!

- Fantasizing in marriage is healthy as long as your mind is filled with pictures of your partner.

- When you disagree with one another, say, "I see things differently, but maybe I can learn from you."

- Ask your partner, "What do you want to be doing five years from now and how can I help you achieve that?"

- Being a friend with your partner means sharing the conversations you have in your mind.

- Some couples don't celebrate their wedding anniversary each year, they celebrate it each month.

- Be conscious of what you pray for. Are your prayers in keeping with the nature of God or are you asking Him to violate His nature if He gives you what you're asking for?

- Does your fiancé know you well enough to write your biography from the age of one to fifteen? If not, begin sharing. You don't want to marry a stranger.

- Do either of you tend to use the words, "If only…"? If so they can immobilize you and lead to worry. Substitute the words, "Let's commit this to the Lord."

- When you have an important decision to make, first pray for wisdom and then ask your fiancé's opinion.

- Doing things for and with your fiancé was part of the process of falling in love—and it's how you'll stay in love.

- "If you love someone, you will be loyal to him no matter what the cost. You will always believe in him, always expect the best of him, and always stand your ground in defending him" (1 Corinthians 13:7, TLB).

𝒬UESTIONS FOR 𝒞OMMITMENT

For You: What advice would you give to another person to build a marriage relationship?

For You and Your Fiancé: Which five of the preceding statements will help you the most? List them in order of importance.

For God: Ask Him to show which of the preceding steps He wants you to implement.

LOVE IS...

❧ ❧ ❧

But the greatest of these is love.

1 CORINTHIANS 13:13

I'm sure you've read 1 Corinthians 13. In fact, many couples
have it included as part of their wedding service.

But few have considered what it means in day-to-day living.
The following paraphrase may help you think about living this
passage out in your forthcoming marriage:

> If I go to language school and learn to speak a hun-
> dred different languages, preach to thousands all over
> the world, and lead all to Christ, but have hate in my
> heart in a silent war with my neighbor who's built his
> privacy fence on my side of the boundary line, my
> words are nothing except the screaming of a heavy
> metal rock band.

> If I have a doctorate in theology, science, language arts,
> and literature and can raise mountains out of the dust
> of the plains, but am only concerned about the size of
> my paycheck, wardrobe, and house, it is as if I don't
> exist…have never existed.

> If I give up a good salary opportunity to work in com-
> passionate ministries, tithe ten percent, give the rest
> to the poor and eventually die for them, but only do
> it to get my name in the paper, and I lose sight of lost
> hungry souls, I certainly don't gain anything but lose
> my own soul.

Love walks the floor all night with a crying baby, smiles as she greets new visitors in Sunday school. She doesn't want what she doesn't have. She doesn't say, "Look how wonderful I am" but "Look how great you are." She doesn't snub anyone, isn't always looking in the mirror, and doesn't make a mental list for retribution when things don't go her way. She doesn't close herself in but opens her heart and makes herself vulnerable to others.

Love remains while the world crumbles around her.

The only things that are really important are faith in God, hope for the future, and love from God for every man. But you cannot have faith or hope until you first understand and demonstrate love.

I can work with the poor like Mother Teresa, write literature like C.S. Lewis, sing like Sandi Patty, move people like Gloria Gaither, preach like Billy Graham, have spiritual insight like James Dobson, be a great leader like Martin Luther King, Jr. and a martyr like Gandhi, but until I love like Jesus my soul is lost.[36]

$\mathcal{Q}$UESTIONS FOR $\mathcal{C}$OMMITMENT

For You: If you were to paraphrase one section from this passage that would improve about your relationship, what would that be?

For You and Your Fiancé: Discuss which part of this paraphrase resonated the most for you and the reason.

For God: Ask Him to enlighten you as to which verse is needed more in your life at the present time.

"AFFLUENZA"—
A DEADLY DISEASE

❧ ❧ ❧

Don't weary yourself trying to get rich.
Why waste your time?

PROVERBS 23:4 TLB

*I*t's predictable. It really is. The major conflict of most couples during the first year is predictable. It's spelled M-O-N-E-Y. Will you follow the pattern of most couples? You don't have to if you take steps to avoid a major disease. It's not small pox or anthrax. It's a disease that's been around for thousands of years. It sounds like influenza. For many it's fatal.

In the 1918–1919 influenza pandemic, millions of people died. While couples are still affected by influenza epidemics today, they're at a higher risk of another epidemic...*affluenza*. That's right, affluenza, not influenza—and it's contagious! Here are the symptoms:

- Desiring to have more, regardless of what we have

- Striving to be successful without being content

- Placing career over family

- Refusing to be satisfied with less than the best

- Refusing to follow the biblical guidelines to live our lives to God's glory[37]

Most people today value what they don't have more than what they do have.

They look at what their friends have and say, "We need that." Some people "need" to buy lots of clothes. Others "need" the latest model car. Still others "must have" the computer with the latest chips and software. But the truth is we don't need it—we *want* it. God's Word has something to say about our need to accumulate things:

> Those who love money will never have enough. How absurd to think that wealth brings true happiness! (Ecclesiastes 5:10, NLT).

> People who long to be rich fall into temptation and are trapped by many foolish and harmful desires that plunge them into ruin and destruction (1 Timothy 6:9, NLT).

> No one can serve two masters. For you will hate one and love the other, or be devoted to one and despise the other. You cannot serve both God and money (Luke 16:13, NLT).

Our contact with the values of our culture alone puts us in danger of catching affluenza, even within our church. You'll need to be on guard, to inoculate yourself against this illness. Part of the inoculation comes from taking an honest look at where you are and understanding that accumulating things doesn't truly satisfy your desires.

One last suggestion. Get some plastic surgery! That's right! Plastic surgery. Get out the scissors and cut up your credit cards. Don't use them for the first year of marriage. Use cash and checks. After the first year bring one back and treat it as a small lovable pet. Don't let it turn into a killer shark![38]

QUESTIONS FOR COMMITMENT

For You: Look again at the symptoms. Can you identify any that you struggle with?

For You and Your Fiancé: Discuss together what you can do during the first year of your marriage to keep from falling into the trap of affluenza. Why not talk about tithing?

For God: Ask Him to guide you in the use of your money for your wedding as well as the future.

YOU'RE GOING
TO BE STRETCHED

*He who covers over an offense promotes love, but who-
ever repeats the matter separates close friends.*

PROVERBS 17:9

*Y*our marriage will stretch you. Some days you will feel
pulled one way and then another. You may even wonder,
"Is this what I signed up for?" Those who have the greatest difficulty are the ones who are rigid and unbending. They're brittle
and in time a crack appears and they break. Other marriages go
with the flow, bend a bit, and move on. They have a crucial ingredient. It's called rubber.

All marriages need to have the qualities of rubber. First of all,
rubber is *resilient* and *elastic*. It bounces back when stress bends
it out of shape, and it expands to fit irregular surfaces. You will
need to do that with each other. Sometimes your partner will
seem to be strangely inconsiderate and irrational. It's true. You
need to bounce back from the hurts and disappointments
inevitable in any close relationship, realizing that no one (you or
your partner) is perfect. (But you've discovered that by now,
haven't you?) The love that underlies a marital commitment can
stretch around bumps in the road.

Rubber also *erases* mistakes. In marriages, you've got to be
ready to forgive the mistakes and hurts inflicted by your partner.
(In this process, the flexible quality of rubber also comes into
play.) But forgiveness is not a whitewash based on the pretense

that either the wrong didn't happen or that it didn't matter to the one that's hurt. There's a distinction between "forgiveness" and "reconciliation." You can forgive your partner without their participation if you conduct a transaction between yourself and God, letting go of your bitterness or hurt toward your partner. But reconciliation requires the participation of both of you. You resume normal relations only after the other who has inflicted the hurt acknowledges his or her wrong and repents. That means saying, "I was wrong" in one way or another, as well as a statement "I won't do it again."

And for reconciliation to occur, you need to indicate what you would do differently if you had the situation to live over again. (P.S. The injured party must also be willing to acknowledge that he or she is not entirely blameless.) Without this kind of rethinking, you leave the door open for the likelihood of a repeat performance. [39]

QUESTIONS FOR COMMITMENT

For You: List two ways you need to be more like the quality of rubber. You know...flexible and resilient.

For You and Your Fiancé: Discuss how you could help one another apply this passage of Scripture.

For God: Ask Him to help you not only be more flexible but be willing to say, "I was wrong. Here's what I will do differently."

There Are
No Shortcuts

Everyone who competes in the games goes into strict training. They do it to get a crown that will not last; but we do it to get a crown that will last forever.

1 Corinthians 9:25

For some men and women, shortcuts are a part of their lives. If they can save time or energy by eliminating some steps in the process, they'll do it. We're encouraged to take shortcuts. Listen to all the "get rich quick" schemes you hear about. Why do we get hooked into those "lose 30 pounds in 30 days" diet schemes? Would we bite if the offer was "lose 30 pounds in 90 days?" Not likely. What about "learn how to speak a foreign language fluently in just 16 easy at-home audio lessons—nothing to read either!" Why take two years of college classes when you can do it in one-tenth the time?

Perhaps you've taken a shortcut while hiking or driving only to discover it took you twice as long to get there. That's the problem with many shortcuts. They don't work. They're often longer in the long run or you bypassed or left out some essentials. Even though you got there, or finished much sooner, you weren't well equipped.

Scripture illustrates the fact that to attain you have to train. There are no shortcuts to Christian growth. It's training, and this means work, diligence, sweat, persistence, and practice.

Why do we take shortcuts? To save time, effort, and even money. You may be tempted to do this in planning for your wedding. Some couples do it for their honeymoon plans only to discover they shortchanged themselves.

It's the same way in marriage. There are no shortcuts to having a fulfilling marriage. You have to put in the hours of conversation, the consistency of being attentive and sensitive to build a closeness. It won't happen overnight. And you can't read "30 days to super sex and super marriage" to substitute for training. Quality marriages are built on foundations that avoid looking at the clock as well as the pocketbook. It may be cheaper to read a book on marriage but it won't have the same effect as a weekend marriage enrichment experience. You do get what you pay for as well as invest in.

So when tempted to cut corners in giving time and attention to one another...don't. It's a good way to get lost in your marriage.[40]

Questions for Commitment

For You: What are some shortcuts you've taken in life and what were the results?

For You and Your Fiancé: Discuss tendencies you've seen to take shortcuts in your relationship. What have been the results?

For God: Ask Him for the strength to follow through in all of your commitments.

PRAYING FOR
YOUR FIANCÉ

❧ ❧ ❧

Pray continually.

1 THESSALONIANS 5:17

*R*ecently I found a fascinating resource that personalizes passages of Scripture into prayer for a husband and wife. It's called *Praying God's Will for My Marriage* by Lee Roberts. Roberts takes passages of Scripture (NKJV) and rewords them. By reading these aloud for a while, anyone can learn to do this for themselves. Here is a sampling (I've changed the word *spouse* to *fiancé*):

> I pray that my fiancé and I will be swift to hear, slow to speak, slow to wrath; for the wrath of man does not produce the righteousness of God (James 1:19-20).

> I pray that my fiancé and I will always love the Lord our God with all our heart, with all our soul, with all our mind, and with all our strength and that we love our neighbor as ourselves (Mark 12:30-31).

> I pray that when my fiancé and I face an obstacle we always remember that God has said, "Not by might nor by power, but by my Spirit" (Zechariah 4:6).

> I pray that if my fiancé and I lack wisdom, we ask it of You, God, who gives to all liberally and without reproach and that it will be given to us (James 1:5).

I pray that my fiancé and I will bless You, the Lord, at all times; and that Your praise will continually be in our mouths (Psalm 34:1).

I pray to You, God, that my fiancé and I will present our bodies a living sacrifice, holy and acceptable to God, which is our reasonable service. I pray also that we will not be conformed to this world, but transformed by the renewing of our minds, that we may prove what is that good and acceptable and perfect will of God (Romans 12:1-2).[41]

As you read these what kind of response did you experience? This is probably a new experience for you. It could be pleasant or uncomfortable. What would happen if you held hands and alternately read each of these phrases out loud to one another?

What other passages would you like to pray as a couple? Can you imagine the effect on your relationship when you use God's Word as prayer? Try this as a one-month experiment. Then note the difference.

Questions for Commitment

For You: Which passages of Scripture would you choose to pray at this time that would benefit your relationship?

For You and Your Fiancé: Discuss your comfort level of praying in this way or of discussing spiritual matters.

For God: Ask Him to direct you to several passages to pray during the first year of marriage in order to give you a stable first year.

A WORD TO
THE WISE

❧ ❧ ❧

*Already you have all that you want! Already you have
become rich! You have become kings—and that without us!
How I wish that you really had become kings so that we
might be kings with you! For it seems to me that God has
put us apostles on display at the end of the procession, like
men condemned to die in the arena. We have been made
a spectacle to the whole universe, to angels as well as to men.*

1 CORINTHIANS 4:8-9

*D*o you know what happens to many couples during the first
three years of marriage? It's the "D" word. *Disenchantment!*
But have you considered that a certain amount of disenchantment
is healthy? One of the earliest marriage specialists wrote this a
number of years ago.

> Disenchantment is healthy, for courtship is the condi-
> tion of simulated perfection, a game well played by par-
> ticipants who can still choose the times and conditions
> favorable to its success. Obviously husbands and wives
> will find communication blocked if they demand a con-
> tinuance of this courtship level of perfection. "We talk
> the same language" is a courtship discovery; a marriage
> discovery is the realization that "talking the same lan-
> guage" only skims the surface of experience. This is all
> laid bare in the disenchantment process.

Right now you may (or may not!) be over-idealizing your
fiancé. Right now you may (or may not!) be on a romantic high.

The more these two factor in, the greater the level of disenchantment you'll experience unless you face reality. And the more mature you are, the more you will accept some disenchantment in your relationship as normal since there will be changes in your situation or behavior that can't be foreseen.

What can be done to guard against radical disenchantment? You may want to consider the following: Don't take shortcuts in your communication. If you talk a lot now, talk a lot after you're married. If you're not much of a talker naturally and you've cranked it up to win your fiancé's love, that could be considered courtship deception. He or she has every right to believe you'll be that way after the wedding.

Avoid being home-centered, children-fixated, and career-oriented to the detriment of your marriage. You may be thinking, "That will *never* happen to us." And it may not but only if you work on not *letting* it happen. You don't want your life to be described as "the ravages of routine." Right now you see being married as being full of bonuses. Don't let them diminish. During courtship you've experienced an excitement of exploring one another's lives. Continue to explore and don't let the enjoyment of being with one another turn into a dim recollection as it has for many couples. You want your marriage to be different and to be alive. It can be. Guard your heart and your marriage against the ravages of the routine.

Questions for Commitment

For You: Describe a time in your life when you experienced disenchantment and how it impacted you.

For You and Your Fiancé: Discuss any feelings of disenchantment you may have experienced so far in your relationship. What will you do to prevent the big "D" from becoming a part of your marriage?

For God: Have you experienced a time of disenchantment with God? Tell Him about this. Ask Him to help you with this feeling.

CHANGE CAN HAPPEN

*Love bears up under anything and everything that
comes, is ever ready to believe the best of every person,
its hopes are fadeless under all circumstances.*

1 CORINTHIANS 13:7 AMP

*A*fter you're married you might someday come to the place
where you think, "nothing can change to improve our relationship." If this ever happens, don't ever believe it. If you do, it
will become a self-fulfilling prophecy. If you or anyone else
believes that nothing can improve your marriage, test this belief.
Challenge it. Look at, define, and clarify some of the problems,
then select one that appears to be the easiest to change.

Haven't you experienced some adjustments already during
your engagement? Probably. Hopefully you found ways to work
through them. If you haven't, what makes you think they'll
change after you're married? When you're married you've got to
believe that each year can be better and stronger than the pre-
vious year. If not, you end up in an ever-deepening rut. Consider
the following example:

One husband just wanted to be able to have discussions with
his wife without defensive arguments that seemed to erupt constantly. This had been the pattern for some time. He learned some
ways he could stay out of the argument and eliminate his defensiveness. This is what he did:

1. He chose to believe that his wife wasn't out to get him
   or simply to argue with him out of spite. She might have
   some good ideas.

101

2. He committed himself not to interrupt her, not to argue or debate, and not to walk out on her.

3. He would respond to what she said by making such statements as "Really," "That's interesting," "I hadn't considered that," "Tell me more," and "I'd like to think about that."

4. He chose to think the following: *Even if this doesn't work the first time, I'll try at least five times.*

5. He determined to thank her for each discussion, and when her response was even five percent less defensive, to compliment her for the way she responded.

Five weeks later he said, "The fourth discussion was totally different. My belief that nothing can improve our relationship is destroyed. There's a bit of hope now." It took action on his part and he believed change could happen.

To counter negative and hopeless beliefs, focus upon passages from God's Word that are future-oriented and filled with hope. For example, in Jeremiah we read, " 'For I know the plans I have for you,' declares the Lord, 'plans for welfare and not for calamity to give you a future and a hope' " (29:11 NASB).[42]

Questions for Commitment

For You: What about you? What would you like to change? The first step may be to change your beliefs.

For You and Your Fiancé: Let one another know the best way to approach you when you would like to see a change occur.

For God: Ask Him to give you a hopeful and positive attitude for future change in the lifetime of your marriage.

WHO'S THE
MOST IMPORTANT?

❦ ❦ ❦

*For by the grace given me I say to every one of you; Do
not think of yourself more highly than you ought, but
rather think of yourself with sober judgment, in accordance with the measure of faith God has given you.*

ROMANS 12:3

*Love each other with brotherly affection and take delight
in honoring each other.*

ROMANS 12:10 TLB

What were your mother's and your father's most important
contributions to their marriage? Did you see one parent
as having a more important role than the other? What about your
future marriage?

Who is going to be the most important person in your marriage? Is it:

- The one who brings home the most money?

- The person who does the majority of the cooking?

- The person who does the laundry?

- The person with the happiest attitude, who lifts everyone
  else's spirits?

- The one who spends the most time in prayer?

Couldn't a case be made for any of these? Sure. We're all good at framing ourselves as the "Truly Indispensable Spouse." My partner really can't get along without me.

Paul throws cold water on that notion. He addresses both spouses—"*to every one of you*." Not just the wives; not just the husbands. *Everybody*.

Each member of a marriage has a role to play. None of us is the whole stage troupe, even though we may like to think so.

Romans 12:10 is about learning to appreciate each other. Beyond the perfunctory "I love you," Paul calls us to genuine affection and enthusiasm about our partner's worth. There's no hint here of competition or power struggle. Your new home is to be a place where each of you is the other's cheerleader.

Read all of Romans 12. Some people think this chapter is unrealistic; life just doesn't work out that way. But wouldn't we like to live in such an atmosphere? Wouldn't it be great? If you as a couple set this ideal before you, could you match up to it for one evening? What about a full day? Then maybe a full weekend? Try it!

If you think a lifestyle of focusing on the other is impossible, it will be. If you think God just might help you make your upcoming marriage more of a delight than a headache, you may be in for a pleasant surprise.[43]

$\mathcal{Q}$UESTIONS FOR $\mathcal{C}$OMMITMENT

For You: Read Romans 12 out loud during your own devotional time. Which verse would really build your present relationship?

For You and Your Fiancé: Read Romans 12 out loud to one another taking turns on each verse. Discuss at least five verses and describe how each verse could impact your relationship.

For God: Ask Him to reveal to you which verses you need to apply more than others.

50/50 OR 100/100?

❧ ❧ ❧

But God demonstrates His own love toward us, in that
while we were yet sinners, Christ died for us.

ROMANS 5:8 NASB

When two people get married, they have expectations how
the relationship should work. Often the unspoken assumption is that "my spouse will meet me halfway." Sometimes it's
called the "50/50 Plan." When the husband and wife operate on
this plan, it's easy for it to spread to other members of the family.[44]

The 50/50 Plan says, "You do your part, and I'll do mine." It
sounds logical, but couples who use it may be surprised.

A young man saw an elderly couple sitting down to lunch at
McDonald's. He noticed that they had ordered one meal and an
extra drink cup. As he watched, the gentleman carefully divided
the hamburger in half, then counted out the fries, one for him,
one for her, until each had half of them. Then he poured half of
the soft drink into the extra cup and set that in front of his wife.
The old man then began to eat, and his wife sat watching, with
her hands folded in her lap. The young man decided to ask if they
would allow him to purchase another meal for them so that they
didn't have to split theirs.

The old gentleman said, "Oh, no. We've been married for 50
years, and everything has always been and will be shared 50/50."

The young man then asked the wife if she was going to eat,
and she replied, "Not yet. It's his turn with the teeth."

Well, the problem with most 50/50 arrangements is that giving is based on merit and performance. There's a focus more on what the other person is giving than on what we are giving. And how do you ever know if your fiancé and future spouse has met you halfway?

Think about the type of love God gives you. No matter what we do, He gives us 100 percent. As Romans 5:8 shows, He gives us love even when we don't deserve it.

There's a better plan. It's called the "100/100 Plan." Give 100 percent no matter what your spouse does. It really does work.[45]

QUESTIONS FOR COMMITMENT

For You: What's been the most difficult area of your relationship when it comes to giving?

For You and Your Fiancé: Discuss these two questions:

1. In what area do you see the other having difficulty in giving?

2. Ask your partner, "How could I assist you in an area that is difficult for you to give?"

For God: Ask Him to show you areas of your life in which you tend to hold back from fully giving to Him.

How Not
to Comfort

*Then Job replied: "I have heard many things like these;
miserable comforters are you all! Will your long-winded
speeches never end?"*

JOB 16:1-3

*Y*ou're having a rotten, lousy day. Nothing has gone right.
One thing after another seems to pile up on you. How could
anyone have so much difficulty at one time? It's like your world
is crumbling around you. Yes, this does happen when you're
engaged and especially in your marriage.

When you've had a rotten day, what do you need from your
fiancé? What do you want when your fiancé has helped you *have*
a rotten day?

Do you have some friends who are around to comfort you?
Who are they? Job had some friends. Or at least he thought they
were his friends. At first, they didn't say anything. They were just
there silently in their support of him, and it helped. Then they
began to talk, and he wished they hadn't. One of them told him
to remember the advice he gave to others in the past. That didn't
help much, but this friend went on with the clincher. He had the
audacity to tell him that he'd had a vision showing him that his
suffering was the result of some sin. Imagine a friend (or your
fiancé) telling you your problems were caused because of some
sin committed! Isn't that great? Then he told you that you
sounded like a fool and what you needed to do was repent. To

make matters worse, he said these problems were blessings in disguise. Great! Just when you needed comfort, empathy and support, what do you get? Theology. And as you argue with your friend or fiancé, their insensitivity grows. It's as though you need to argue with their theology. If this has happened to you, you're not alone. Remember Job? You can read about it in Job 4 and 5.

When someone is hurting, he or she needs comfort, not theology. He or she needs you to listen, not give advice: "Understand [this], my beloved brethren. Let every man be quick to hear [a ready listener], slow to speak" (James 1:19, AMP). Your fiancé doesn't need criticism, he or she needs encouragement. Be there, be silent, be available, be sensitive, be present.

QUESTIONS FOR COMMITMENT

For You: During the time you've been dating your fiancé, what's the worst day you've experienced? What or who helped you the most?

For You and Your Fiancé: After you're married, how do you want your spouse to share with you they've had a terrible day? How would you like to be comforted?

For God: Ask Him for insight and sensitivity so you don't respond like Job's friends.

FOLLOWING JESUS

❧ ❧ ❧

Only conduct yourselves in a manner
worthy of the gospel of Christ.

PHILIPPIANS 1:27 NASB

*𝒥*f you know Jesus Christ as your Savior, you have a potential for experiencing more from life than those who don't know Him. As a follower of Jesus Christ, are you doing what today's verse says in your relationship? Are you following Him in what you do and how you respond to your fiancé? What about you and your parents? Siblings? Those at work? The wedding coordinator? Sales people in the department stores as you set up your registry? Caterers? Yes, this verse applies to every situation you can imagine. Consider these examples from Jesus' life.

Jesus had compassion. We see His compassion expressed in Mark 8:2: "I feel compassion for the people because they have remained with Me now three days and have nothing to eat" (NASB). His concern was to alleviate suffering and meet the needs of the people. In what way have you demonstrated compassion to your fiancé? How would your fiancé like you to respond when he or she is sick, had a bad day at work, etc? Have you ever discussed this question? If not, do so. It beats guessing.

Jesus accepted people. When Jesus first met people, He accepted them as they were. In other words, He believed in them and what they would become. The characteristic of acceptance is seen in John 4, John 8, and Luke 19. When Jesus met the woman at the well, He accepted her as she was without condemning her. He accepted the woman caught in adultery, as He also did with Zacchaeus, the dishonest tax collector. How can you accept others in your life? After you're married who might it be difficult for you to accept?

Jesus gave people worth. People were Jesus' top priority. He established this priority and gave them worth by putting their needs before the rules and regulations the religious leaders had constructed. He involved Himself in the lives of people who were considered the worst of sinners, and He met them where they had a need. In so doing, He helped elevate their sense of self-worth.

One of the ways Jesus gave worth to people was by showing them their value in God's eyes, by comparing God's care for other creatures with God's care for them: "Are not two sparrows sold for a cent? And yet not one of them will fall to the ground apart from your Father" (Matthew 10:29, NASB).

QUESTIONS FOR COMMITMENT

For You: How can you help your fiancé feel more valuable today?

For You and Your Fiancé: Discuss those people in your life who make it difficult to apply this verse. Talk about what you can do about this.

For God: Ask Him for the grace and patience you need to live out this passage of Scripture.

WHAT'S DWELLING IN YOU?

❦ ❦ ❦

Let the word of Christ richly dwell within you.

COLOSSIANS 3:16 NASB

*H*ow many verses of Scripture do you know from memory? The Scripture itself says, "Let the word of Christ richly dwell within you." When a passage is locked in your mind, there's a greater likelihood it will become a part of your behavior. What might your upcoming marriage be like in five years if you and your future spouse memorized just one verse a month during that time? You may be amazed at the results.

Have you ever opened a peach or an apple and found something living in it that you weren't pleased to see? You know what your reaction would be, especially if you had already taken a bite out of it!

At a family gathering, my daughter came in and saw a bowl of the biggest, ripest, juiciest strawberries she'd ever seen. She sat down and started to eat a bowl of them one by one. She bit one in half so when she took what was left out of her mouth and held it in front of her, she could see the inside of the strawberry. There was a little hollowed out space. She noticed a number of little specks like miniature eggs, as well as half an earwig wiggling. It dawned on her where the other half was and with that she ran to the bathroom to spit out the strawberry and crushed remains of the rest of the earwig! That bug had been dwelling, making itself at home, inside the strawberry.

We all have different things dwelling in us. It could be germs. It could be an infection. It could be thoughts and fantasies that hurt our relationship. Paul said there is something that needs to be at home in a husband and wife's life. It's called the Word of God.

How comfortable are you with Scripture being not only in your mind but also directing your life? It may be a new experience, but it can become very comfortable. A lot of people know Ephesians 4:32, "Be kind and compassionate to one another, forgiving each other, just as Christ God forgave you." But living it out is another step. If this passage is really living in a husband and wife, it means it's at home there. It's comfortable. It means each looks at the other and thinks, "How can I be kind and tenderhearted to you today?" What would the answer to that question do for your future marriage?

Questions for Commitment

For You: How can you be kind and tenderhearted this week to: Your fiancé? Your fiancé's family? Your family?

For You and Your Fiancé: Share your thoughts and feelings about memorizing Scripture.

For God: Ask Him to make His Word come alive in your life today.

WHAT DOES
COMMITMENT MEAN?

❦ ❦ ❦

*For this reason a man will leave his father and
mother and be united to his wife, and the two will
become one flesh.*

MATTHEW 19:5

*D*o you realize how long people live in this country? Seventy,
eighty, or even ninety years. Think about this: If you're in
your twenties or thirties, when you complete your wedding
vows with your fiancé you're committing yourself to at least
fifty years to that person. A half a century! Are you ready for that
commitment?

Did you know the word "commitment" is not used in the
Bible, but its derivatives "committed" and "commit" are. Commitment has two meanings in the Greek: "doing or practicing
something" and "delivering or entrusting something to a person."
Commitment involves the binding or pledging of oneself to a par-
ticular course of action. It also implies a choice based on reasoning (not just emotion). The act of entrusting oneself to another
should be supported by sound reasoning. Men and women
should be able to offer themselves and others sound, rational
arguments for why their marriages will be healthy and should be
expected to flourish. Commitment also involves consent; persons
will themselves into relationships. When the will to relate to
another person is supported by reasons that validate the good-
ness or the fit, then we may reasonably expect to see a stable,
long-term relationship. (Do you have a list of those reasons?)

Commitment implies a pledge by each spouse to fidelity for life. When commitment is present, a couple enters into an irrevocable covenant. They pledge their faithfulness, regardless of circumstances. It has something of the spirit of Hernando Cortez when, in 1519, he landed his troops at Vera Cruz, Mexico. The more than 6,000 men were irrevocably committed to their task of conquering the new land for the mother country. When Cortez set fire to the vessels that brought them, there was no retreat. That kind of "no retreat" commitment in marriage is indicated in the verse for today.

Commitment is the unconditional acceptance of the other partner. Commitment is the surrender of personal pleasure and comfort.

Commitment costs something; dependability has a price tag. Consistently encouraging a partner, giving the gifts of sympathetic understanding, and saying no to personal desires cuts against the grain of the selfish nature. Commitment means organizing one's time, thoughts, and resources for the benefit of others. It means the surrender of a measure of personal freedoms and rights.[46]

QUESTIONS FOR COMMITMENT

For You: What are the commitments that you have made in your lifetime?

For You and Your Fiancé: Discuss your thoughts and feelings about commitment and what it means to your marriage.

For God: Ask for His strengths and wisdom to keep the commitments in your life.

Marriage and
the Stock Market

✢ ✢ ✢

Love…is not self-seeking…love…
always hopes, always perseveres.

1 Corinthians 13:4,7

*D*o you invest in the stock market? If not now, someday you might. It's not for the faint-hearted since there can be daily fluctuations in stock prices. Investors tend to do best when they don't react to the day-to-day swings in prices. Those who are glued to the daily reports to see what their funds are doing and constantly move their investments in and out of the market don't do as well in the long run. Why? The long-term growth is compromised. Losses are greater for the movers than those who, regardless of the market, keep on investing.

Whether it's stocks, mutual funds, savings accounts, or CDs, those who end up doing the best are the long-term investors.[47]

One of the reasons you're on the verge of marriage is an investment in a relationship. You put in time, effort, adjusted schedules, learned how to give, and love in a new way. This seems to be an investment that's going to pay some significant dividends.

The authors of *A Lasting Promise* described your pending marriage in this way:

> Think of your marriage as a long-term investment. The ups and downs in the stock market and the value of a good mutual fund are like the ups and downs of satisfaction in marriage. These ups and downs are

inevitable and normal. Unending bliss is just not what marriage is like for most people. It's wonderful at times and very hard at times—and sometimes it's wonderfully hard. In good marriages, satisfaction can be down for long periods of time, only to rebound later to mutual joy—just like the stock market. If you get too focused on the down cycles, you can bail out too quickly and lose much of what you've invested. Successful couples just keep on investing, whether the relationship feels great or lousy. That's why it takes commitment—a long-term view.[48]

One other factor. Talk to an investment expert and you'll hear the advice: Diversity. In marriage those who do well have learned to multiply a number of ways they invest within the relationship. Share with one another in many ways—sexually, recreationally, intellectually, teamwork in problem-solving. In each of these you're connecting, but in a different way. This is diversification. Remember: "diversified investment is the key to preventing erosion in your commitment."[49]

Questions for Commitment

For You: In what way could you invest more in your relationship?

For You and Your Fiancé: Ask one another, "In what area of our relationship would you like to see me invest more?"

For God: Ask God for an awareness of where you might be holding back in your relationship.

A Marriage Based
on One Verse

❧ ❧ ❧

*Be kind and compassionate to one another, forgiving
each other, just as in Christ God forgave you.*

EPHESIANS 4:32

*W*hat a verse to help couples! How can we apply it in the
daily living between a couple about to be married? And
how can we apply it to the daily living between a husband and
wife? Here are some possibilities:

Cancel debts. Forgiving other people just as God in Christ has
forgiven us means canceling the debts. It means resisting the
impulse to bring up the past. It may mean asking our fiancé to
forgive us if we bring up old problems on impulse in the heat of
an argument. Unfortunately, some people in marriage are more
than financial debt collectors. They're personal debt collectors.
If Jesus canceled your debts, follow His lead.

Be kind. Webster's dictionary defines kindness as being sympathetic, gentle, and benevolent. Forgiveness springs much easier
from an attitude of kindness than from an attitude of defensiveness. When we feel threatened, we naturally get defensive.
Replacing defensiveness with kindness means we become vulnerable to being taken advantage of again. That's why being
kind is sometimes difficult. It takes a strong person to be gentle,
and sometimes we don't feel all that strong. But we are called by
Scripture to be kind, so we are promised strength as well. Psalm
28:7 says, "The Lord is my strength and my shield; my heart trusts

in Him, and I am helped; therefore my heart exults, and with my song I shall thank Him" (NASB).

Be tenderhearted. Being kind implies some vulnerability, but being tenderhearted implies even more vulnerability. It means absorbing some hurts so your fiancé can grow. It means letting our walls down and inviting our partners to feel our emotions with us. It also means feeling their emotions with them. When we are tenderhearted, it becomes much easier to forgive.

The opposite of tenderheartedness is hardness of heart. In Mark 10:4-5, Jesus says hardness of heart was the reason Moses wrote the law on divorce. In other words, tenderhearted couples don't need divorce. Tenderhearted people can forgive. No one has found a better way to live yet.

QUESTIONS FOR COMMITMENT

For You: Can you identify a personal debt you would like canceled at this time in your life in any relationship? What are three acts of kindness you could perform today toward your fiancé and his or her parents?

For You and Your Fiancé: Discuss how you would like your fiancé to be even gentler than they are at this time in your relationship. How could each of you be kinder at this time toward both sets of parents?

For God: Ask Him to create in you a desire to fulfill this verse toward everyone you come in contact with during the planning for your wedding.

WHERE IS HE?

᯽ ᯽ ᯽

You made all the delicate, inner parts of my body, and knit them together in my mother's womb. Thank you for making me so wonderfully complex! It is amazing to think about. Your workmanship is marvelous—and how well I know it. You were there while I was being formed in utter seclusion! You saw me before I was born and scheduled each day of my life before I began to breathe. Every day was recorded in your book!

PSALMS 139:13-16 TLB

*D*o you have a Palm Pilot or a Day-Timer? If so, do you live by it or let it guide your life? Is it filled at this time with appointments for your wedding?

More and more we seem to be in a society that reminds us of an upcoming appointment. You make an appointment at the dentist's office, and they call the day before to remind you. You make an appointment at the hairdresser's, and they call the day before to remind you. You make an appointment at the counselor's office, and they call the day before to remind you. It's getting to be the same for the wedding dress consultant, as well as the caterer.

Why? It's simple. This is also the age of "no shows" for appointments. And when that happens, there's a vacancy in someone's schedule. That means lost income.

At sports events, when stating the attendance, announcers usually talk about the number of "no shows."

Some couples feel there's been a "no show" in their marriage in some ways. Sometimes discouraged couples say God was a "no show" in their marriages. They wonder where He was and is! One or both are waiting for God to show up. But surprise of all surprises—God is always there in their marriages, as He will be in yours.

The two of you didn't meet by chance. He knew each of you long before you were born.

God was there watching when you first met.

God knew your thoughts about each other. (As He does today.)

He was there at your first kiss as He was when one of you popped the question.

God will be in attendance at your wedding as well as there for your wedding night. He will be there blessing your marriage and desiring the best for you. He is there even now, even though you can't see Him or feel Him.

You don't have to be concerned about God not "showing up." He's never absent. If you ever feel this way, could it be that you just missed Him? You know we might fail to show up in some way because of a lapse in our spiritual life?

So, who's really missing? Hopefully, no one. Enjoy God.[50]

Questions for Commitment

For God: Can you think of times when you felt God was absent and when you felt God was really there?

For You and Your Fiancé: Discuss what you can do to remind yourself that God is always with you.

For God: Ask Him to reveal Himself daily in some new way.

A LOVE
THAT LASTS

❧ ❧ ❧

Love never gives up.

1 CORINTHIANS 13:4 THE MESSAGE

*T*he wonder and the promise of a love that lasts were once
related to me in the writings of an older man. Listen to the
message he gave to all of us as he wrote:

> I couldn't even describe what I thought love was when
> I was first married. Forty years is a long time to be
> together with one person. It's almost half of a century.
> All I knew then was that I wanted a love that would
> keep us together forever. Jean really felt those love feel-
> ings a lot of people talk about. I'm not so sure I did.
> But I knew that I loved her. I still do. That's me all right.
> We learned it's all right to be different in the style of
> love we had and how we expressed it, as long as we
> were adaptable enough to learn to put it into a package
> that the other person liked. I didn't do that the first
> twenty years and that's what created what we now call
> our valley of "love recessions." Sometimes the wick of
> our candle of love got kind of low. But it never went
> out. We learned to work at our love and make it
> stronger. And it works, no matter what anyone says.
>
> Now that we're almost in our seventies we don't know
> how many more years we'll have to love one another.
> But we'll make the most of them. I'm not a poet or
> much of a reader, never have been, but I found a

statement that puts into words some of my thoughts better than I can. Maybe this will have a message to the next generation right behind us.

> It is love in old age, no longer blind, that is true love. For love's highest intensity doesn't necessarily mean its highest quality. Glamour and jealousy are gone; and the ardent caress, no longer needed, is valueless compared to the reassuring touch of a trembling hand. Passersby commonly see little beauty in the embrace of young lovers on a park bench, but the understanding smile of an old wife to her husband is one of the loveliest things in the world.

That sums it all up.[51]

Questions for Commitment

For You: What will it take on your part for you to be able to say what was said here when you're in your seventies?

For You and Your Fiancé: Describe what you thought and what you felt as you read this older man's thoughts.

For God: Thank Him now for the love you have for one another and ask Him to increase this each day.

YOUR SPOUSE,
YOUR ALLY

❧ ❧ ❧

A new command I give you: Love one another. As I have
loved you, so you must love one another. By this all men
will know that you are my disciples, if you love one
another.

JOHN 13:34,35

*I*t's easy to become distracted and concentrate our efforts in
the wrong directions. If you remember your history, you'll
recall studying the War of 1812. It was significant in the history
of our country. Major General Andrew Jackson, the seventh
president of our country, was serving in the Tennessee militia.
During the war, the morale of his troops was terrible. They
argued, bickered, and fought among themselves. One day all of
these problems intensified and General Jackson called the troops
together, looked at them, and said one simple sentence, "Gentleman! Remember, the enemy is over *there!*"

This problem hasn't gone away. We see it today even in the
church. There's arguing, bickering, and infighting all too often.
As Christians we're called to pull for one another, to support one
another, believe in one another, care for one another, pray for one
another, love one another.

There's another place where people sometimes become mis-
directed and bicker, attack, and argue. It's called marriage. A
spouse is not the enemy. Couples are not to see one another as
adversaries, but as allies. In marriage we are to pull for, support,
believe in, care for, pray for, and love one another.

You don't have to wait for marriage for this problem to occur. Right now during your engagement is a prime time for conflicts to erupt. Some of your expectations and plans won't turn out the way you want—someone will cancel, not show, or forget. You and your fiancé, as well as your parents, will have different ideas as to music, wedding cake, who sits where, etc. Have you discovered all of these potential tension situations yet? You will. And this is the best place to practice living out Jesus' teaching.

During the days of the early church, an emperor sent out a man named Aristides to check on a group of people called Christians. He saw them in action and came back with a mixed report. But one statement he made has lasted throughout the centuries: "Behold! How they love one another."

As others look at you an engaged couple and then a married couple, hopefully this is what they say about you.[52]

Questions for Commitment

For You: What makes it difficult for you to respond as this passage teaches?

For You and Your Fiancé: What is a source of tension at this time in your relationship that you need to resolve?

For God: Ask Him to give you a love in your heart for those who are difficult to love at this moment.

THE RHYTHM
OF YOUR MARRIAGE

ᴤᴥ ᴤᴥ ᴤᴥ

Wives, submit to your husbands as to the Lord...Husbands, love your wives, just as Christ loved the church and gave himself up for her.

EPHESIANS 5:22,25

*M*arriage is more than a set of rules and roles. It's got to be. It's true you need to work out who does what and when. It's also true that there must be some division of labor. It's true that you need to discover who has the capability and giftedness in certain areas. (Hopefully someone knows how to cook.) There are many couples who have all of the above worked out, but the way they function is still awkward. They don't work together as a team, but as two disjointed individuals.

Headship and submission are two areas that create tension for many couples. In fact, many couples ignore this passage today. Dr. Larry Crabb says:

> A really good marriage has the feel of a man and woman blending together into natural movement where individuality is obviously present but really isn't the point, something perhaps like dance partners of many years who anticipate each other's steps with practiced ease.
>
> The rhythm of the music and the dancers' movements are two separate ingredients, and although it's clear that one directs the other, you don't sense that the dancers

are working hard to keep in step with the music. The rhythm is *in* them; they move with it naturally, effortlessly, with every movement fitting the music because the music is part of them.

Learning how headship and submission actually work in a marriage is sometimes as clumsy as an inexperienced teenager learning to dance. There are rules to follow, there are roles that lay out the steps to take, but neither rules nor roles creates the awareness of rhythm that makes for good dancing.

There is a rhythm in a relationship, a rhythm that can only be heard as the great truths about God are played over and over again.[53]

Do the two of you dance? If so, how do you look? Smooth or awkward? Have you ever ice-skated with a partner? Those who are proficient are graceful but others are disasters. It takes countless hours of learning to move together and blend into a unit. It's going to be the same way in your marriage. Some think the best way to do this is with structured rules, "You take care of these ten items and I'll handle theses ten tasks." That way everything is covered. Will this work?

Questions for Commitment

For You: In what areas of your relationship do you work together smoothly? In what areas of your relationship do you feel awkward?

For You and Your Fiancé: What do each of you believe about headship and submission? What does it mean to each of you?

For God: Ask Him for guidance as the two of you reflect on Ephesians 5 and 1 Peter 3 as a foundation for your marriage.

SENSITIVE
TO THE EXTREME

જ જ જ

A quick-tempered man does foolish things, and a crafty
man is hated.

PROVERBS 14:17

*Y*ou've met quick-tempered and critical people before. Who
are they? Those people who have the inherent, super-
sensitive antenna sticking out, who interpret whatever you say,
whatever you do, however you look as a personal vendetta
against them. These individuals have the highest refined capability of finding slights, insults, put-downs, and degrading com-
ments where none were ever intended or they just don't exist!
Then they misinterpret and react defensively, aggressively, or
both. You may discover this tendency with some new in-laws
or family friends you inherit. You may discover them at work or
during the wedding preparations.

A critical person demands an apology. And if your response
isn't to his or her satisfaction, watch out. His or her tendency is
to counterattack. An arsenal of weapons is unleashed. The silent
treatment is one of the choices. So is slamming the door, ques-
tioning your parents' abilities as parents, and cutting off inter-
action. Not pleasant people to be around. Sometimes they're
referred to as emotional vampires.

Hopefully you're not an overly sensitive person. Hopefully
your fiancé isn't an overly sensitive person. It's hard enough
contending with a sibling or parent who's this way, let alone

having this happen within marriage. If anyone you know tends to be overly sensitive, what can he or she do? Reflect on these questions and see if either of you tend to be this way:

1. Is there a tendency to imagine the worst or to interpret something as an insult? Can you think of when this has happened in your life?

2. Is the Holy Spirit called upon to bring a balance into the perceptions?

3. Has prayer occurred for a proper response if there has been an offense?

4. Has the offending person been asked, "Could you please clarify that?" or "Could you say that in a different way, please?" (These would be great phrases to use when you're married.)

5. Has the following passage been put into practice? "A man's wisdom gives him patience; it is to his glory to overlook an offense" (Proverbs 19:11).

Instead of assuming the worst, assume the best. It's a totally different outcome![54]

QUESTIONS FOR COMMITMENT

For You: How do you pray when your fiancé has offended you?

For You and Your Fiancé: What would be the best way for each of you to respond when either you feel you've been hurt or the other person is angry?

For God: Ask Him to give you patience with others and a clear understanding any time you're angry.

A Prayer for
Your Marriage

※ ※ ※

*Therefore, I urge you, brothers, in view of God's mercy,
to offer your bodies as living sacrifices, holy and pleasing
to God—this is your spiritual act of worship.*

ROMANS 12:1

*H*ere's a prayer for your marriage. You may want to read it out loud:

Dear God,

I'm praying today for wisdom to know what I need to be doing as I prepare for my marriage.

Help me to overcome my not wanting to face any truth, which I need to face. Sometimes it's hard to hear the truth from my fiancé and future life partner.

I need help in overcoming hesitancy that keeps me from learning the truth.

Help me to overcome any stubbornness that keeps me from accepting the truth, especially in my own family.

I really need strength to overcome pride that keeps me from looking for and accepting the truth.

Keep my eyes and ears open so I can hear You speak to my conscience as well as my heart.

Take away any blockage in my life which would keep me from accepting advice especially from my fiancé.

Open up my mind, which at times resists what my partner suggests and even resists the Holy Spirit, the Spirit of truth.

Give me the grace and power to do what I know I ought to do in my relationship today as well as my forthcoming marriage.

Lord, keep me from getting off course. Help me with my lack of resistance which might give into temptation all too easily.

Help me to overcome procrastination of the things I know are needed.

Give me the perseverance to complete the tasks that are important to my fiancé.

So now once again I ask for wisdom to know Your will and do it.

In Jesus' name, amen.[55]

Questions for Commitment

For You: If you were to add to this prayer, what would you ask for?

For You and Your Fiancé: Which of these prayer requests need to be addressed at this time?

For God: Ask Him to show you specific areas for growth in your relationship.

MAKE THE MOST
OF YOUR TIME

✦ ✦ ✦

Consider it all joy...when you encounter
various trials, knowing that the testing
of your faith produces endurance.

JAMES 1:2,3 NASB

*B*y now, you're much closer to your wedding date; I'd like
to share with you the story of one of my closest friend's
marriage. He was 53 and his wife was 40. He has a message for
the two of you:

> My wife and I met through the Internet but really it was
> through a lot of prayer. God just used that to allow us
> to find each other. We both had been looking a long
> time for that right person but never seemed to find the
> "right one." That was until I got an e-mail from a nurse
> in San Diego asking me to write her because she
> thought we might have a number of things in common.
> I did and I could tell from her correspondence that her
> heart was very sincere and I had found a very special
> lady. After writing and talking on the phone for what
> seemed like weeks, we met in Julian where she was on
> a church retreat for the weekend. She proceeded to tell
> me as we walked and talked that while praying, Jesus
> had told her that I was going to marry her. I looked at
> her a little surprised and told her that He hadn't told
> me that...and she said..."Have you asked Him?"

We had such a great first date that we decided to get together again the next day and go for a walk on the beach...which she took me to her favorite beach...Del Mar. After walking a while on the beach, she told me that she wanted to show me around other parts of Del Mar, so we continued to walk. We went past beautiful parks, art galleries, food places...then we came to this beautiful church and walked around admiring all the stained glass in it. She then told me, "I would love to get married some day in this church." Not realizing that this was the church she already attended and had so many friends there, I told her, "That's nice." Well, six months later we were married...in that church... and yes, Jesus did tell me that she was the one.

Dale and Sherry expected to be married for many years. Neither expected her to develop lung cancer.

Sherry loved being married. She loved me so deeply she wanted to beat this terrible disease trying every treatment possible. She spent a long time with God daily asking Him to heal her if it was His will...but God had other plans for her.

What Sherry and I had in the three and a half years together is packed with so many memories. We thought we were making up for things we missed out on in the past. We didn't realize we were doing things for the future we wouldn't have together. We had a wonderful time and life together and neither of us would have changed it for anything. I would do it over again in a second if God gave me that chance. If there is one thing from this tragedy that could be passed on to any couple, it would be to enjoy every minute you have together...as it could be your last.

Questions for Commitment

For You and Your Fiancé: How will you make the most of your time when you are married? Remember the last paragraph of this story. It may help you to cherish your time together.

For God: Allow us to cherish every moment we have together.

POSTSCRIPT

❧ ❧ ❧

You've finished this book. You've started on the journey of building your spiritual intimacy. Where do you go from here? I'd like to suggest, as you start married life, that you begin with *Quiet Times for Couples*. This resource has been used by more than a half-million couples. And who knows, you may receive one as a wedding gift.

When you've completed *Quiet Times,* there's another resource just waiting for you. The *After You Say I Do* devotional. You'll find 365 different devotionals directly related to your marriage. Some of which I used in this book.

And one last request. For years I've enjoyed receiving wedding announcements from couples who have used my materials. If you would like to send one, here's the address:

H. Norman Wright
P.O. Box 2468
Orange, CA 92859
1-800-875-7560

And may God bless you in your marriage.

NOTES

❧ ❧ ❧

1. Scott Stanley, Ph.D., *The Heart of Commitment* (Nashville: Thomas Nelson, 1998), pp. 186-87.
2. Tim Clinton and Julie Clinton, *The Marriage You've Always Wanted* (Nashville, TN: Word, 2000), pp. 14-15.
3. Ibid., pp. 27-28.
4. Ibid., adapted, p. 26-28.
5. Stephen Covey, *The Seven Habits of Highly Effective People* (New York: Simon & Schuster, 1989), pp. 30-31.
6. Clinton, *The Marriage You've Always Wanted,* pp. 97-98.
7. Samuel Beckett, *Waiting for Godot* (New York: Grove, 1954), p. 32
8. Steve and Valerie Bell, *Made to Be Loved* (Chicago: Moody Press, 1999), adapted, pp. 53-55.
9. Ibid., p.129-30.
10. Ibid., p. 30.
11. Ibid., adapted, p. 31.
12. Les and Leslie Parrott, *Getting Ready for the Wedding* (Grand Rapids, MI: Zondervan Publishers, 1998), p. 19.
13. Ibid., adapted, pp. 31-32, by Dave and Claudia Arp.
14. Ibid., p. 32, by Dave and Claudia Arp.
15. Gordon MacDonald, *Restoring Your Spiritual Passion* (Nashville: Thomas Nelson, 1986), adapted, pp. 96-104.
16. Charles R. Swindoll, *The Finishing Touch* (Dallas: Word, Inc., 1994), p. 281.
17. Dr. Richard Matteson and Janis Long Harris, *What if I Married the Wrong Person?* (Minneapolis: Bethany House Publishers, 1997), adapted, pp. 236-38.
18. Tom Marshall, *Right Relationships* (Kent, England: Sovereign World, 1992), adapted, pp. 43-46.
19. Charles Swindoll, *Hope Again* (Dallas: Word, 1996), adapted, pp. 119-27
20. Gregory K. Popcak, MSW, *The Exceptional Seven Percent* (New York: Kensington Publishing Corp., 2000), p. 165.
21. Ibid., p. 169.
22. Bill and Pam Farrell, *Love to Love You* (Eugene, OR: Harvest House, 1997), pp. 34-35, 38-39.

23. Ibid., pp. 12-13.

24. Dr. Gary and Barbara Rosberg, *The 5 Love Needs of Men and Women* (Wheaton, IL: Tyndale House, 2000), pp. 57, 59-60.

25. Ibid., adapted, pp. 77, 81.

26. David Keirsey and Marilyn Bates, *Please Understand Me* (Del Mar, CA: Prometheus Nemesis Books, 1978), p. 1.

27. Les and Leslie Parrott, *Becoming Soul Mates* (Grand Rapids, MI: Zondervan, 1995), p. 17.

28. Thomas F. Jones, *Sex and Love When You're Single Again* (Nashville, TN: Thomas Nelson Publishers, 1990), adapted, pp. 93-96.

29. Dr. Neil Clark Warren, *Finding the Love of Your Life* (Colorado Springs, CO: Focus on the Family, 1992), pp. 81, 82.

30. James Patterson and Peter Kim, *The Day America Told the Truth* (New York: Prentice Hall, 1991), adapted, pp. 45, 49.

31. Joseph Aldrich, *Secrets to Inner Beauty* (Santa Barbara, CA: Vision House, 1977), pp. 87-88.

32. Philip Yancey, *I Was Just Wondering* (Grand Rapids, MI: Eerdmans, 1989), pp. 174-75.

33. Swindoll, *Hope Again,* pp. 99-100.

34. Bob and Cheryl Moeller, *Marriage Minutes* (Chicago: Moody Press, 1998), adapted, Oct.14-16.

35. Gary Rosberg, *Guard Your Heart* (Sisters, OR: Multnomah Press, 1994), adapted, pp. 24-27.

36. Angela McCord, student paper, quoted by Les and Leslie Parrot, *Becoming Soul Mates* (Grand Rapids, MI: Zondervan, 1995), pp. 36-37.

37. Steve Farrar, *If I'm Not Tarzan and My Wife Isn't Jane, Then What Are We Doing in the Jungle?* (Portland, OR: Multnomah, 1991), adapted, pp. 65-66.

38. Dave Ramsey, *Financial Peace* (New York: Viking, 1997), adapted, p. 77.

39. Dennis and Ruth Gibson, *The Sandwich Years* (Grand Rapids, MI: Baker Book House, 1991), pp. 162-63.

40. Shawn Craig, *Between Sundays* (West Monroe, LA: Howard Publishing, 1998), adapted, p. 263.

41. Lee Roberts, *Praying God's Will for My Marriage* (Nashville: Thomas Nelson, 1994), pp. 1, 9, 19, 28, 102, 115, 227, 267.

42. H. Norman Wright, *Secrets of a Lasting Marriage* (Ventura, CA: Regal Books, 1995), adapted, p. 87.

43. Dean Merrill, *Wait Quietly,* (Wheaton, IL: Tyndale House, 1991), adapted, pp. 186-87.

44. Dennis and Barbara Rainey, *Moments Together for Couples* (Ventura, CA: Regal Books, 1995), adapted, March 21.

45. Rainey, adapted, March 21.

46. Ronald E. Hawkins, *Marital Intimacy* (Grand Rapids, MI: Baker Book House, 1991), adapted, pp. 35-36.

47. Scott Stanley, Daniel Trathen, Savanna McCain and Milt Bryan, *A Lasting Promise* (San Francisco, CA: Josey-Bass, 1998), adapted, pp. 181-82.

48. Ibid., p. 182.

49. Ibid., p. 183.

50. Bell, *Made to Be Loved,* adapted, pp. 53-55.

51. Original source unknown.

52. Swindoll, *Hope Again,* adapted, pp. 45-46.

53. Larry Crabb, *Men and Women* (Grand Rapids, MI: Zondervan, 1991), pp. 299, 211, 212.

54. Jim Smoke, *Facing 50* (Nashville: Thomas Nelson, 1994), adapted, pp. 40, 41.

55. William Barclay, *A Barclay Prayer Book* (London: SCM Press Ltd., 1963), adapted, pp. 28-29.

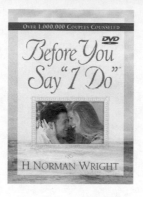

Packed with biblical wisdom, insightful questions, and real-life examples, six 25-minute sessions explore role expectations, communication, sexuality, in-laws, and more.

Bestselling author and marriage counselor Norm Wright draws from his many years of experience to help couples

- adjust to differences in personality and background
- clarify role expectations
- develop their spiritual lives
- establish a positive sexual relationship
- talk over how to handle finances

As couples discover the role that Jesus Christ has in their relationship, they will gain what they need to make their marriage all it's meant to be.

- *Includes helpful guide for leaders, counselors, and couples*
- *Bonus 15-minute session: "On Your First Anniversary"*

ISBN 978-0-7369-2752-9